MORE PROMISES
FROM GOD FOR
WOMEN
OF COLOR

More Promises from God for Women of Color

Copyright 2021

Published By: Urban Spirit
Atlanta, Georgia
New York, New York
Chicago, Illinois

Editorial Production by Livingstone, LLC.
Cover and interior design by Larry P. Taylor

Scripture Quotations are taken from the Holy Bible King James Version

Produced by: American Bible Company

Presented to

....

Date

....

By

....

Table of Contents

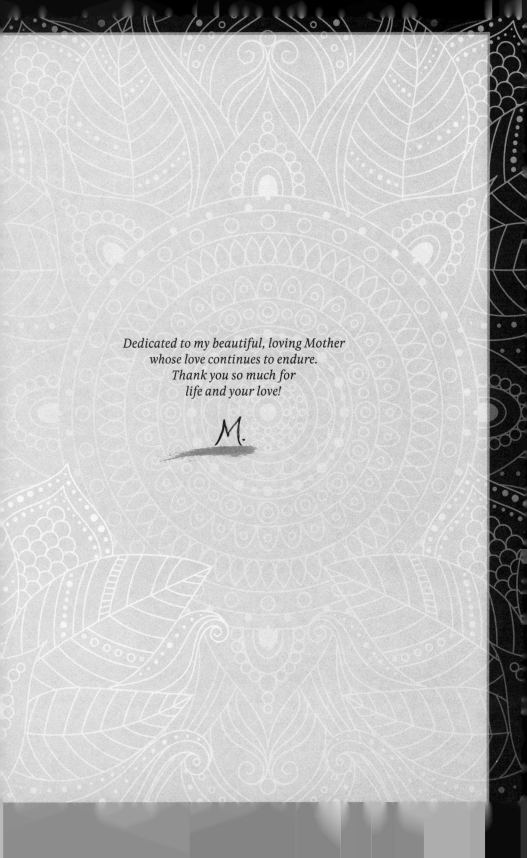

Dedicated to my beautiful, loving Mother
whose love continues to endure.
Thank you so much for
life and your love!

M.

Assurance

Snuggle in God's arms... When you are hurting, when you feel lonely, left out, let Him cradle you, comfort you, reassure you of His all sufficient power and love.

Kay Arthur

John 10: 27 -29
Jesus said, "My sheep hear my voice, and I know them, and they follow me:
And I give unto them eternal life; and they shall never perish, neither shall any man pluck them out of my hand. My Father, which gave them me, is greater than all; and no man is able to pluck them out of my Father's hand".

Acts 17: 31
Because he hath appointed a day, in the which he will judge the world in righteousness by that man whom he hath ordained; whereof he hath given assurance unto all men, in that he hath raised him from the dead.

Isaiah 32: 17
And the work of righteousness shall be peace; and the effect of righteousness quietness and assurance for ever.

John 5: 24
Verily, verily, I say unto you, He that heareth my word, and believeth on him that sent me, hath everlasting life, and shall not come into condemnation; but is passed from death unto life.

Isaiah 54: 10
For the mountains shall depart, and the hills be removed; but my kindness shall not depart from thee, neither shall the covenant of my peace be removed, saith the Lord that hath mercy on thee.

Psalm 34: 4
I sought the Lord, and he heard me, and delivered me from all my fears.

Philippians 4: 6 - 7
Be careful for nothing; but in every thing by prayer and supplication with thanksgiving let your requests be made known unto God. And the peace of God, which passeth all understanding, shall keep your hearts and minds through Christ Jesus.

Psalm 73: 23 -26
Nevertheless I am continually with thee: thou hast holden me by my right hand. Thou shalt guide me with thy counsel, and afterward receive me to glory. Whom have I in heaven but thee? and there is none upon earth that I desire beside thee. My flesh and my heart faileth: but God is the strength of my heart, and my portion for ever.

Psalm 46: 10 - 11

Be still, and know that I am God: I will be exalted among the heathen, I will be exalted in the earth. The Lord of hosts is with us; the God of Jacob is our refuge. Selah.

Isaiah 41: 13

For I the Lord thy God will hold thy right hand, saying unto thee, Fear not; I will help thee.

Romans 8: 35, 37 -39

Who shall separate us from the love of Christ? shall tribulation, or distress, or persecution, or famine, or nakedness, or peril, or sword? Nay, in all these things we are more than conquerors through him that loved us. For I am persuaded, that neither death, nor life, nor angels, nor principalities, nor powers, nor things present, nor things to come, Nor height, nor depth, nor any other creature, shall be able to separate us from the love of God, which is in Christ Jesus our Lord.

Psalm 56: 4

In God I will praise his word, in God I have put my trust; I will not fear what flesh can do unto me.

1 Peter 5: 6 - 7

Humble yourselves therefore under the mighty hand of God, that he may exalt you in due time: Casting all your care upon him; for he careth for you.

2 Timothy 1: 12

For the which cause I also suffer these things: nevertheless I am not ashamed: for I know whom I have believed, and am persuaded that he is able to keep that which I have committed unto him against that day.

Psalm 55: 22
Cast thy burden upon the Lord, and he shall sustain thee: he shall never suffer the righteous to be moved.

Matthew 6 : 25 - 29
Jesus said, "Therefore I say unto you, Take no thought for your life, what ye shall eat, or what ye shall drink; nor yet for your body, what ye shall put on. Is not the life more than meat, and the body than raiment? Behold the fowls of the air: for they sow not, neither do they reap, nor gather into barns; yet your heavenly Father feedeth them. Are ye not much better than they? Which of you by taking thought can add one cubit unto his stature? And why take ye thought for raiment? Consider the lilies of the field, how they grow; they toil not, neither do they spin: And yet I say unto you, That even Solomon in all his glory was not arrayed like one of these.

John 16: 33
These things I have spoken unto you, that in me ye might have peace. In the world ye shall have tribulation: but be of good cheer; I have overcome the world.

Psalm 31: 13 - 14
For I have heard the slander of many: fear was on every side: while they took counsel together against me, they devised to take away my life.

Psalm 37: 4 -5
Delight thyself also in the Lord; and he shall give thee the desires of thine heart.
Commit thy way unto the Lord; trust also in him; and he shall bring it to pass.

Acts 2: 38 - 39

Then Peter said unto them, Repent, and be baptized every one of you in the name of Jesus Christ for the remission of sins, and ye shall receive the gift of the Holy Ghost. For the promise is unto you, and to your children, and to all that are afar off, even as many as the Lord our God shall call.

Psalm 103: 11- 12

For as the heaven is high above the earth, so great is his mercy toward them that fear him. As far as the east is from the west, so far hath he removed our transgressions from us.

2 Corinthians 1: 20 -22

For all the promises of God in him are yea, and in him Amen, unto the glory of God by us. Now he which stablisheth us with you in Christ, and hath anointed us, is God; Who hath also sealed us, and given the earnest of the Spirit in our hearts.

Matthew 5: 18 - 19

For verily I say unto you, Till heaven and earth pass, one jot or one tittle shall in no wise pass from the law, till all be fulfilled. Whosoever therefore shall break one of these least commandments, and shall teach men so, he shall be called the least in the kingdom of heaven: but whosoever shall do and teach them, the same shall be called great in the kingdom of heaven.

Proverbs 3: 24 - 26

When thou liest down, thou shalt not be afraid: yea, thou shalt lie down, and thy sleep shall be sweet. Be not afraid of sudden fear, neither of the desolation of the wicked, when it cometh. For the Lord shall be thy confidence, and shall keep thy foot from being taken.

Blessings

New day, new Blessing. Don't let yesterdays failures ruin the beauty of today, because each day has its own promise of love, joy, and forgiveness.
Good Morning

– Onuh Justus Izuchukwu

1 Timothy 1: 14
And the grace of our Lord was exceeding abundant with faith and love which is in Christ Jesus.

Ezekiel 34: 26
And I will make them and the places round about my hill a blessing; and I will cause the shower to come down in his season; there shall be showers of blessing.

Psalm 5: 12
For thou, Lord, wilt bless the righteous; with favour wilt thou compass him as with a shield.

John 10: 10

The thief cometh not, but for to steal, and to kill, and to destroy: I am come that they might have life, and that they might have it more abundantly.

Psalm 36: 7 -8

How excellent is thy lovingkindness, O God! therefore the children of men put their trust under the shadow of thy wings. They shall be abundantly satisfied with the fatness of thy house; and thou shalt make them drink of the river of thy pleasures.

Romans 8: 28

And we know that all things work together for good to them that love God, to them who are the called according to his purpose.

2 Corinthians 8: 9

Wherefore I beseech you that ye would confirm your love toward him. For to this end also did I write, that I might know the proof of you, whether ye be obedient in all things.

Matthew 5: 3 - 10

Blessed are the poor in spirit: for theirs is the kingdom of heaven. Blessed are they which are persecuted for righteousness' sake: for theirs is the kingdom of heaven.

Ephesians 1 : 3

Blessed be the God and Father of our Lord Jesus Christ, who hath blessed us with all spiritual blessings in heavenly places in Christ:

Ephesians 3: 20-21

Now unto him that is able to do exceeding abundantly above all that we ask or think, according to the power that worketh in us, Unto him be glory in the church by Christ Jesus throughout all ages, world without end. Amen.

Psalms 37: 11
But the meek shall inherit the earth; and shall delight themselves in the abundance of peace.

Matthew 13: 12
For whosoever hath, to him shall be given, and he shall have more abundance: but whosoever hath not, from him shall be taken away even that he hath.

Deuteronomy 16: 15
Seven days shalt thou keep a solemn feast unto the Lord thy God in the place which the Lord shall choose: because the Lord thy God shall bless thee in all thine increase, and in all the works of thine hands, therefore thou shalt surely rejoice.

Psalm 118: 26
Blessed be he that cometh in the name of the Lord: we have blessed you out of the house of the Lord.

Psalm 37: 11
But the meek shall inherit the earth; and shall delight themselves in the abundance of peace.

Mathew 13: 12
For whosoever hath, to him shall be given, and he shall have more abundance: but whosoever hath not, from him shall be taken away even that he hath.

Psalm 118: 26
Blessed be he that cometh in the name of the Lord: we have blessed you out of the house of the Lord.

Psalm 29: 11
The Lord will give strength unto his people; the Lord will bless his people with peace.

Celebration

*"The triumph can't be had
without the struggle."*

– Wilma Rudolph

Isaiah 12: 2 - 6
Behold, God is my salvation; I will trust, and not be afraid: for the Lord Jehovah is my strength and my song; he also is become my salvation. Therefore with joy shall ye draw water out of the wells of salvation. And in that day shall ye say, Praise the Lord, call upon his name, declare his doings among the people, make mention that his name is exalted. Sing unto the Lord; for he hath done excellent things: this is known in all the earth. Cry out and shout, thou inhabitant of Zion: for great is the Holy One of Israel in the midst of thee.

Isaiah 61: 10

I will greatly rejoice in the Lord, my soul shall be joyful in my God; for he hath clothed me with the garments of salvation, he hath covered me with the robe of righteousness, as a bridegroom decketh himself with ornaments, and as a bride adorneth herself with her jewels.

Exodus 15: 1 - 2

Then sang Moses and the children of Israel this song unto the Lord, and spake, saying, I will sing unto the Lord, for he hath triumphed gloriously: the horse and his rider hath he thrown into the sea. The Lord is my strength and song, and he is become my salvation: he is my God, and I will prepare him an habitation; my father's God, and I will exalt him.

Isaiah 65: 17 -19

For, behold, I create new heavens and a new earth: and the former shall not be remembered, nor come into mind. But be ye glad and rejoice for ever in that which I create: for, behold, I create Jerusalem a rejoicing, and her people a joy. And I will rejoice in Jerusalem, and joy in my people: and the voice of weeping shall be no more heard in her, nor the voice of crying.

Psalm 149: 3 - 4

Let them praise his name in the dance: let them sing praises unto him with the timbrel and harp. For the Lord taketh pleasure in his people: he will beautify the meek with salvation.

Psalm 16: 8 - 9

I have set the Lord always before me: because he is at my right hand, I shall not be moved. Therefore my heart is glad, and my glory rejoiceth: my flesh also shall rest in hope.

Isaiah 35: 10
And the ransomed of the Lord shall return, and come to Zion with songs and everlasting joy upon their heads: they shall obtain joy and gladness, and sorrow and sighing shall flee away.

Psalm 30: 11 - 12
Thou hast turned for me my mourning into dancing: thou hast put off my sackcloth, and girded me with gladness; To the end that my glory may sing praise to thee, and not be silent. O Lord my God, I will give thanks unto thee for ever.

Psalm 47: 1 - 2
O clap your hands, all ye people; shout unto God with the voice of triumph. For the Lord most high is terrible; he is a great King over all the earth.

Comfort

"We will be ourselves and free,
or die in the attempt. Harriet Tubman was not
our great-grandmother for nothing."

– Alice Walker

Psalm 23: 4
Yea, though I walk through the valley of the shadow of death, I will fear no evil: for thou art with me; thy rod and thy staff they comfort me.

2 Corinthians 1: 3 - 5
Blessed be God, even the Father of our Lord Jesus Christ, the Father of mercies, and the God of all comfort; Who comforteth us in all our tribulation, that we may be able to comfort them which are in any trouble, by the comfort wherewith we ourselves are comforted of God. For as the sufferings of Christ abound in us, so our consolation also aboundeth by Christ.

Nahum 1: 7
The Lord is good, a strong hold in the day of trouble; and he knoweth them that trust in him.

Psalm 138: 7
Though I walk in the midst of trouble, thou wilt revive me: thou shalt stretch forth thine hand against the wrath of mine enemies, and thy right hand shall save me.

John 14: 15 - 16
If ye love me, keep my commandments. And I will pray the Father, and he shall give you another Comforter, that he may abide with you for ever;

Romans 15: 4
For whatsoever things were written aforetime were written for our learning, that we through patience and comfort of the scriptures might have hope.

Isaiah 42: 6
I the Lord have called thee in righteousness, and will hold thine hand, and will keep thee, and give thee for a covenant of the people, for a light of the Gentiles;

Psalm 34: 18
The Lord is nigh unto them that are of a broken heart; and saveth such as be of a contrite spirit.

Isaiah 66: 13 - 14
As one whom his mother comforteth, so will I comfort you; and ye shall be comforted in Jerusalem. And when ye see this, your heart shall rejoice, and your bones shall flourish like an herb: and the hand of the Lord shall be known toward his servants, and his indignation toward his enemies.

John 14: 26
But the Comforter, which is the Holy Ghost, whom the Father will send in my name, he shall teach you all things, and bring all things to your remembrance, whatsoever I have said unto you.

Psalm 34: 17
The righteous cry, and the Lord heareth, and delivereth them out of all their troubles. Deuteronomy 31: 8

Luke 6: 22
Blessed are ye, when men shall hate you, and when they shall separate you from their company, and shall reproach you, and cast out your name as evil, for the Son of man's sake.

Psalm 27: 13 - 14
I had fainted, unless I had believed to see the goodness of the Lord in the land of the living. Wait on the Lord: be of good courage, and he shall strengthen thine heart: wait, I say, on the Lord.

Psalm 34: 4
I sought the Lord, and he heard me, and delivered me from all my fears.

Isaiah 40: 10 - 11
Behold, the Lord God will come with strong hand, and his arm shall rule for him: behold, his reward is with him, and his work before him. He shall feed his flock like a shepherd: he shall gather the lambs with his arm, and carry them in his bosom, and shall gently lead those that are with young.

Psalm 147: 3
He healeth the broken in heart, and bindeth up their wounds.

John 14: 18 - 19
I will not leave you comfortless: I will come to you. Yet a little while, and the world seeth me no more; but ye see me: because I live, ye shall live also.

Psalm 46: 1
God is our refuge and strength, a very present help in trouble.

Psalm 9: 9
The Lord also will be a refuge for the oppressed, a refuge in times of trouble.

Psalm 119: 76 - 77
Let, I pray thee, thy merciful kindness be for my comfort, according to thy word unto thy servant. Let thy tender mercies come unto me, that I may live: for thy law is my delight.

Psalm 34: 19
Many are the afflictions of the righteous: but the Lord delivereth him out of them all.

Isaiah 43: 2 - 3
When thou passest through the waters, I will be with thee; and through the rivers, they shall not overflow thee: when thou walkest through the fire, thou shalt not be burned; neither shall the flame kindle upon thee. For I am the Lord thy God, the Holy One of Israel, thy Saviour: I gave Egypt for thy ransom, Ethiopia and Seba for thee.

Isaiah 57: 15
For thus saith the high and lofty One that inhabiteth eternity, whose name is Holy; I dwell in the high and holy place, with him also that is of a contrite and humble spirit, to revive the spirit of the humble, and to revive the heart of the contrite ones.

Commitment

"You're not obligated to win. You're obligated to keep trying to do the best you can every day."

– Marian Wright Edelman

Mathew 16: 24 - 25
Then said Jesus unto his disciples, If any man will come after me, let him deny himself, and take up his cross, and follow me. For whosoever will save his life shall lose it: and whosoever will lose his life for my sake shall find it.

1 Thessalonians 5: 21, 23 - 24
Prove all things; hold fast that which is good. And the very God of peace sanctify you wholly; and I pray God your whole spirit and soul and body be preserved blameless unto the coming of our Lord Jesus Christ. Faithful is he that calleth you, who also will do it.

2 John 8 - 9

Look to yourselves, that we lose not those things which we have wrought, but that we receive a full reward. Whosoever transgresseth, and abideth not in the doctrine of Christ, hath not God. He that abideth in the doctrine of Christ, he hath both the Father and the Son.

Mathew 7: 24 - 25

Therefore whosoever heareth these sayings of mine, and doeth them, I will liken him unto a wise man, which built his house upon a rock: And the rain descended, and the floods came, and the winds blew, and beat upon that house; and it fell not: for it was founded upon a rock.

Galatians 6: 9

And let us not be weary in well doing: for in due season we shall reap, if we faint not.

Ephesians 6: 5 - 8

Not with eyeservice, as menpleasers; but as the servants of Christ, doing the will of God from the heart; With good will doing service, as to the Lord, and not to men: Knowing that whatsoever good thing any man doeth, the same shall he receive of the Lord, whether he be bond or free.

Proverbs 16: 3

Commit thy works unto the Lord, and thy thoughts shall be established.

Psalms 37: 4 - 5
Delight thyself also in the Lord; and he shall give thee the desires
of thine heart.
Commit thy way unto the Lord; trust also in him; and he shall
bring it to pass.

Revelations 3: 11 - 12
Behold, I come quickly: hold that fast which thou hast, that no
man take thy crown. Him that overcometh will I make a pillar
in the temple of my God, and he shall go no more out: and I will
write upon him the name of my God, and the name of the city
of my God, which is new Jerusalem, which cometh down out of
heaven from my God: and I will write upon him my new name.

James 1: 25
But whoso looketh into the perfect law of liberty, and continueth
therein, he being not a forgetful hearer, but a doer of the work,
this man shall be blessed in his deed.

Confidence

"Self-esteem means knowing you are the dream."

– Oprah Winfrey

Psalm 31: 24
Be of good courage, and he shall strengthen your heart, all ye that hope in the Lord.

Hebrews 13: 5 - 6
Let your conversation be without covetousness; and be content with such things as ye have: for he hath said, I will never leave thee, nor forsake thee. So that we may boldly say, The Lord is my helper, and I will not fear what man shall do unto me.

2 Corinthians 3: 4 -5
And such trust have we through Christ to God-ward: Not that we are sufficient of ourselves to think any thing as of ourselves; but our sufficiency is of God;

Proverbs 3: 25 - 26
Be not afraid of sudden fear, neither of the desolation of the wicked, when it cometh. For the Lord shall be thy confidence, and shall keep thy foot from being taken.

Psalm 28: 7
The Lord is my strength and my shield; my heart trusted in him, and I am helped: therefore my heart greatly rejoiceth; and with my song will I praise him.

Isaiah 41: 10
Fear thou not; for I am with thee: be not dismayed; for I am thy God: I will strengthen thee; yea, I will help thee; yea, I will uphold thee with the right hand of my righteousness.

Psalm 18: 28 - 29
For thou wilt light my candle: the Lord my God will enlighten my darkness. For by thee I have run through a troop; and by my God have I leaped over a wall.

Isaiah 32: 17
And the work of righteousness shall be peace; and the effect of righteousness quietness and assurance for ever.

Psalm 56: 3 - 4
What time I am afraid, I will trust in thee. In God I will praise his word, in God I have put my trust; I will not fear what flesh can do unto me.

Psalm 18: 32 - 33
It is God that girdeth me with strength, and maketh my way perfect. He maketh my feet like hinds' feet, and setteth me upon my high places.

Isaiah 43: 2 - 3

He shall not cry, nor lift up, nor cause his voice to be heard in the street. A bruised reed shall he not break, and the smoking flax shall he not quench: he shall bring forth judgment unto truth.

Psalm 27: 1- 3

The Lord is my light and my salvation; whom shall I fear? the Lord is the strength of my life; of whom shall I be afraid? When the wicked, even mine enemies and my foes, came upon me to eat up my flesh, they stumbled and fell. Though an host should encamp against me, my heart shall not fear: though war should rise against me, in this will I be confident.

Encouragement

"Give light and people will find the way."

– Ella Baker

Psalm 68: 19
Blessed be the Lord, who daily loadeth us with benefits, even the God of our salvation. Selah.

Luke 6: 21
Blessed are ye that hunger now: for ye shall be filled. Blessed are ye that weep now: for ye shall laugh.

Psalm 94: 18 - 19
When I said, My foot slippeth; thy mercy, O Lord, held me up. In the multitude of my thoughts within me thy comforts delight my soul.

Psalm 25: 1- 2
Unto thee, O Lord, do I lift up my soul. O my God, I trust in thee: let me not be ashamed, let not mine enemies triumph over me.

2 Corinthians 4: 16 - 17

For which cause we faint not; but though our outward man perish, yet the inward man is renewed day by day. For our light affliction, which is but for a moment, worketh for us a far more exceeding and eternal weight of glory;

Mathew 11: 28 - 29

Come unto me, all ye that labour and are heavy laden, and I will give you rest. Take my yoke upon you, and learn of me; for I am meek and lowly in heart: and ye shall find rest unto your souls.

2 Thessalonians 2: 16 - 17

Now our Lord Jesus Christ himself, and God, even our Father, which hath loved us, and hath given us everlasting consolation and good hope through grace, Comfort your hearts, and stablish you in every good word and work.

John 16: 33

These things I have spoken unto you, that in me ye might have peace. In the world ye shall have tribulation: but be of good cheer; I have overcome the world.

Psalm 43: 5

Why art thou cast down, O my soul? and why art thou disquieted within me? hope in God: for I shall yet praise him, who is the health of my countenance, and my God.

Isaiah 65: 23 - 24

They shall not labour in vain, nor bring forth for trouble; for they are the seed of the blessed of the Lord, and their offspring with them. And it shall come to pass, that before they call, I will answer; and while they are yet speaking, I will hear.

Isaiah 49: 4

Then I said, I have laboured in vain, I have spent my strength for nought, and in vain: yet surely my judgment is with the Lord, and my work with my God.

Lamentations 3: 21 - 23

This I recall to my mind, therefore have I hope. It is of the Lord's mercies that we are not consumed, because his compassions fail not. They are new every morning: great is thy faithfulness.

2 Chronicles 15: 7

Be ye strong therefore, and let not your hands be weak: for your work shall be rewarded.

Psalm 147: 3

He healeth the broken in heart, and bindeth up their wounds.

John 8: 12

Then spake Jesus again unto them, saying, I am the light of the world: he that followeth me shall not walk in darkness, but shall have the light of life.

Lamentations 3: 25

It is good that a man should both hope and quietly wait for the salvation of the Lord.

James 4: 8

Draw nigh to God, and he will draw nigh to you. Cleanse your hands, ye sinners; and purify your hearts, ye double minded.

Evangelism

here are two ways of spreading light - to be the candle or the mirror that reflects it.

—Edith Wharton

Romans 1: 16
For I am not ashamed of the gospel of Christ: for it is the power of God unto salvation to every one that believeth; to the Jew first, and also to the Greek.

Mathew 5: 16
Let your light so shine before men, that they may see your good works, and glorify your Father which is in heaven.

1 Timothy 4: 13 - 15
Till I come, give attendance to reading, to exhortation, to doctrine. Neglect not the gift that is in thee, which was given thee by prophecy, with the laying on of the hands of the presbytery. Meditate upon these things; give thyself wholly to them; that thy profiting may appear to all.

Mark 13: 10 - 11

And the gospel must first be published among all nations. But when they shall lead you, and deliver you up, take no thought beforehand what ye shall speak, neither do ye premeditate: but whatsoever shall be given you in that hour, that speak ye: for it is not ye that speak, but the Holy Ghost.

Mathew 28: 18 - 20

And Jesus came and spake unto them, saying, All power is given unto me in heaven and in earth. Go ye therefore, and teach all nations, baptizing them in the name of the Father, and of the Son, and of the Holy Ghost: Teaching them to observe all things whatsoever I have commanded you: and, lo, I am with you alway, even unto the end of the world Amen.

Ephesians 4: 11 - 13

And he gave some, apostles; and some, prophets; and some, evangelists; and some, pastors and teachers; For the perfecting of the saints, for the work of the ministry, for the edifying of the body of Christ: Till we all come in the unity of the faith, and of the knowledge of the Son of God, unto a perfect man, unto the measure of the stature of the fulness of Christ:

John 3: 16 - 17

For God so loved the world, that he gave his only begotten Son, that whosoever believeth in him should not perish, but have everlasting life. For God sent not his Son into the world to condemn the world; but that the world through him might be saved.

Luke 14: 12 - 14

Then said he also to him that bade him, When thou makest a dinner or a supper, call not thy friends, nor thy brethren, neither thy kinsmen, nor thy rich neighbours; lest they also bid thee again, and a recompence be made thee. But when thou makest a feast, call the poor, the maimed, the lame, the blind: And thou shalt be blessed; for they cannot recompense thee: for thou shalt be recompensed at the resurrection of the just.

2 Corinthians 5: 17 - 19

Therefore if any man be in Christ, he is a new creature: old things are passed away; behold, all things are become new. And all things are of God, who hath reconciled us to himself by Jesus Christ, and hath given to us the ministry of reconciliation; To wit, that God was in Christ, reconciling the world unto himself, not imputing their trespasses unto them; and hath committed unto us the word of reconciliation.

Faith

"You are on the eve of a complete victory. You can't go wrong. The world is behind you."

– Josephine Baker

Ephesians 1: 13 - 14
In whom ye also trusted, after that ye heard the word of truth, the gospel of your salvation: in whom also after that ye believed, ye were sealed with that holy Spirit of promise, Which is the earnest of our inheritance until the redemption of the purchased possession, unto the praise of his glory.

Galatians 3: 26
For ye are all the children of God by faith in Christ Jesus.

Psalm 9: 10
And they that know thy name will put their trust in thee: for thou, Lord, hast not forsaken them that seek thee.

1 John 5: 4 - 5
For whatsoever is born of God overcometh the world: and this is the victory that overcometh the world, even our faith. Who is he that overcometh the world, but he that believeth that Jesus is the Son of God?

Mathew 17: 20
And Jesus said unto them, Because of your unbelief: for verily I say unto you, If ye have faith as a grain of mustard seed, ye shall say unto this mountain, Remove hence to yonder place; and it shall remove; and nothing shall be impossible unto you.

Psalm 26: 1
Judge me, O Lord; for I have walked in mine integrity: I have trusted also in the Lord; therefore I shall not slide.

John 14: 12
Verily, verily, I say unto you, He that believeth on me, the works that I do shall he do also; and greater works than these shall he do; because I go unto my Father.

Psalm 57: 1- 2
Be merciful unto me, O God, be merciful unto me: for my soul trusteth in thee: yea, in the shadow of thy wings will I make my refuge, until these calamities be overpast. I will cry unto God most high; unto God that performeth all things for me.

Isaiah 26: 3 - 4
Thou wilt keep him in perfect peace, whose mind is stayed on thee: because he trusteth in thee. Trust ye in the Lord for ever: for in the Lord Jehovah is everlasting strength:

Proverbs 30: 5
Every word of God is pure: he is a shield unto them that put their trust in him.

Ephesians 2: 8 - 9
For by grace are ye saved through faith; and that not of yourselves: it is the gift of God:
Not of works, lest any man should boast.

Jeremiah 17: 7
Blessed is the man that trusteth in the Lord, and whose hope the Lord is.

Proverbs 29: 25
The fear of man bringeth a snare: but whoso putteth his trust in the Lord shall be safe.

Hebrews 11: 1
Now faith is the substance of things hoped for, the evidence of things not seen.

Psalm 37: 3
Trust in the Lord, and do good; so shalt thou dwell in the land, and verily thou shalt be fed.

Psalm 28: 7
The Lord is my strength and my shield; my heart trusted in him, and I am helped: therefore my heart greatly rejoiceth; and with my song will I praise him.

Psalm 125: 1
They that trust in the Lord shall be as mount Zion, which cannot be removed, but abideth for ever.

Psalm 32: 10
Many sorrows shall be to the wicked: but he that trusteth in the Lord, mercy shall compass him about.

Hebrews 11: 16
But now they desire a better country, that is, an heavenly: wherefore God is not ashamed to be called their God: for he hath prepared for them a city.

Psalm 34: 8 - 9
O taste and see that the Lord is good: blessed is the man that trusteth in him. O fear the Lord, ye his saints: for there is no want to them that fear him.

Romans 5: 1 - 2
Therefore being justified by faith, we have peace with God through our Lord Jesus Christ: By whom also we have access by faith into this grace wherein we stand, and rejoice in hope of the glory of God.

Proverbs 16: 20
He that handleth a matter wisely shall find good: and whoso trusteth in the Lord, happy is he.

Proverbs 28: 26
He that trusteth in his own heart is a fool: but whoso walketh wisely, he shall be delivered.

Psalm 37: 40
And the Lord shall help them and deliver them: he shall deliver them from the wicked, and save them, because they trust in him.

family

A family tie is like a tree,
it can bend but it cannot break.

~ African proverb.

Ephesians 3: 14 - 16
For this cause I bow my knees unto the Father of our Lord Jesus Christ, Of whom the whole family in heaven and earth is named, That he would grant you, according to the riches of his glory, to be strengthened with might by his Spirit in the inner man;

1 John 3: 1 - 2
Behold, what manner of love the Father hath bestowed upon us, that we should be called the sons of God: therefore the world knoweth us not, because it knew him not. Beloved, now are we the sons of God, and it doth not yet appear what we shall be: but we know that, when he shall appear, we shall be like him; for we shall see him as he is.

Psalm 68: 5
A father of the fatherless, and a judge of the widows, is God in his holy habitation.

Psalm 107: 41 - 43
Yet setteth he the poor on high from affliction, and maketh him families like a flock. The righteous shall see it, and rejoice: and all iniquity shall stop her mouth. Whoso is wise, and will observe these things, even they shall understand the lovingkindness of the Lord.

Isaiah 38: 19
The living, the living, he shall praise thee, as I do this day: the father to the children shall make known thy truth.

Hebrews 2: 16 - 18
For verily he took not on him the nature of angels; but he took on him the seed of Abraham. Wherefore in all things it behoved him to be made like unto his brethren, that he might be a merciful and faithful high priest in things pertaining to God, to make reconciliation for the sins of the people. For in that he himself hath suffered being tempted, he is able to succour them that are tempted.

2 Corinthians 6: 17 - 18
Wherefore come out from among them, and be ye separate, saith the Lord, and touch not the unclean thing; and I will receive you, And will be a Father unto you, and ye shall be my sons and daughters, saith the Lord Almighty.

Deuteronomy 4: 40
Thou shalt keep therefore his statutes, and his commandments, which I command thee this day, that it may go well with thee, and with thy children after thee, and that thou mayest prolong thy days upon the earth, which the Lord thy God giveth thee, for ever.

Isaiah 54: 13
And all thy children shall be taught of the Lord; and great shall be the peace of thy children.

Proverbs 29: 17
Correct thy son, and he shall give thee rest; yea, he shall give delight unto thy soul.

Mathew 18: 2, 4
And Jesus called a little child unto him, and set him in the midst of them, Whosoever therefore shall humble himself as this little child, the same is greatest in the kingdom of heaven.

Deuteronomy 30: 9
And the Lord thy God will make thee plenteous in every work of thine hand, in the fruit of thy body, and in the fruit of thy cattle, and in the fruit of thy land, for good: for the Lord will again rejoice over thee for good, as he rejoiced over thy fathers:

Psalm 133: 1
Behold, how good and how pleasant it is for brethren to dwell together in unity!

Ephesians 6: 4
And, ye fathers, provoke not your children to wrath: but bring them up in the nurture and admonition of the Lord.

Proverbs 22: 6
Train up a child in the way he should go: and when he is old, he will not depart from it.

Psalm 127: 3 - 5
Children are an heritage of the Lord: and the fruit of the womb is his reward. As arrows are in the hand of a mighty man; so are children of the youth. Happy is the man that hath his quiver full of them: they shall not be ashamed, but they shall speak with the enemies in the gate.

Psalm 102: 28
The children of thy servants shall continue, and their seed shall be established before thee.

Deuteronomy 7: 13
And he will love thee, and bless thee, and multiply thee: he will also bless the fruit of thy womb, and the fruit of thy land, thy corn, and thy wine, and thine oil, the increase of thy kine, and the flocks of thy sheep, in the land which he sware unto thy fathers to give thee.

Proverbs 17: 6
Children's children are the crown of old men; and the glory of children are their fathers.

Ephesians 6: 1 - 3

Children, obey your parents in the Lord: for this is right. Honour thy father and mother; (which is the first commandment with promise;) That it may be well with thee, and thou mayest live long on the earth.

Psalm 128: 1 - 3

Blessed is every one that feareth the Lord; that walketh in his ways. For thou shalt eat the labour of thine hands: happy shalt thou be, and it shall be well with thee. Thy wife shall be as a fruitful vine by the sides of thine house: thy children like olive plants round about thy table.

forgiveness

*"Whatever someone did to you in the past
has no power over the present.
Only you give it power."*

— Oprah Winfrey

Micah 7: 18
Who is a God like unto thee, that pardoneth iniquity,
and passeth by the transgression of the remnant of his
heritage? he retaineth not his anger for ever, because he
delighteth in mercy.

1 John 1: 9
If we confess our sins, he is faithful and just to forgive us
our sins, and to cleanse us from all unrighteousness.

Psalm 103: 12
As far as the east is from the west, so far hath he removed
our transgressions from us.

Mathew 6:14
For if ye forgive men their trespasses, your heavenly Father will also forgive you:

Isaiah 1:18
Come now, and let us reason together, saith the Lord: though your sins be as scarlet, they shall be as white as snow; though they be red like crimson, they shall be as wool.

Proverbs 19:11
The discretion of a man deferreth his anger; and it is his glory to pass over a transgression.

Isaiah 43:25
I, even I, am he that blotteth out thy transgressions for mine own sake, and will not remember thy sins.

Galatians 2:13 - 14
And the other Jews dissembled likewise with him; insomuch that Barnabas also was carried away with their dissimulation. But when I saw that they walked not uprightly according to the truth of the gospel, I said unto Peter before them all, If thou, being a Jew, livest after the manner of Gentiles, and not as do the Jews, why compellest thou the Gentiles to live as do the Jews?

Psalm 12:1
Help, Lord; for the godly man ceaseth; for the faithful fail from among the children of men.

Jeremiah 33: 8
And I will cleanse them from all their iniquity, whereby they have sinned against me; and I will pardon all their iniquities, whereby they have sinned, and whereby they have transgressed against me.

Psalm 86: 5
For thou, Lord, art good, and ready to forgive; and plenteous in mercy unto all them that call upon thee.

Proverbs 17: 9
He that covereth a transgression seeketh love; but he that repeateth a matter separateth very friends.

Nehemiah 9: 17
And refused to obey, neither were mindful of thy wonders that thou didst among them; but hardened their necks, and in their rebellion appointed a captain to return to their bondage: but thou art a God ready to pardon, gracious and merciful, slow to anger, and of great kindness, and forsookest them not.

Ephesians 1: 7 - 8
In whom we have redemption through his blood, the forgiveness of sins, according to the riches of his grace; Wherein he hath abounded toward us in all wisdom and prudence;

2 Corinthians 5: 17 - 19

Therefore if any man be in Christ, he is a new creature: old things are passed away; behold, all things are become new. And all things are of God, who hath reconciled us to himself by Jesus Christ, and hath given to us the ministry of reconciliation; To wit, that God was in Christ, reconciling the world unto himself, not imputing their trespasses unto them; and hath committed unto us the word of reconciliation.

Ephesians 4: 32

And be ye kind one to another, tenderhearted, forgiving one another, even as God for Christ's sake hath forgiven you.

Luke 6: 37

Judge not, and ye shall not be judged: condemn not, and ye shall not be condemned: forgive, and ye shall be forgiven:

Generosity

*"There is always something to do.
There are hungry people to feed,
naked people to clothe, sick people to comfort
and make well. And while I don't expect you to save
the world I do think it's not asking too much for you
to love those with whom you sleep,
share the happiness of those whom you call friend,
engage those among you who are visionary
and remove from your life those who offer you
depression, despair and disrespect."*

– Nikki Giovanni

2 Corinthians 9: 6 - 7

But this I say, He which soweth sparingly shall reap also sparingly; and he which soweth bountifully shall reap also bountifully. Every man according as he purposeth in his heart, so let him give; not grudgingly, or of necessity: for God loveth a cheerful giver.

Luke 6: 38

Give, and it shall be given unto you; good measure, pressed down, and shaken together, and running over, shall men give into your bosom. For with the same measure that ye mete withal it shall be measured to you again.

Acts 20: 35

I have shewed you all things, how that so labouring ye ought to support the weak, and to remember the words of the Lord Jesus, how he said, It is more blessed to give than to receive.

Malachi 3: 10

Bring ye all the tithes into the storehouse, that there may be meat in mine house, and prove me now herewith, saith the Lord of hosts, if I will not open you the windows of heaven, and pour you out a blessing, that there shall not be room enough to receive it.

Hebrews 13: 2

Be not forgetful to entertain strangers: for thereby some have entertained angels unawares.

Romans 8: 32

He that spared not his own Son, but delivered him up for us all, how shall he not with him also freely give us all things?

Psalm 112: 5 - 6

A good man sheweth favour, and lendeth: he will guide his affairs with discretion. Surely he shall not be moved for ever: the righteous shall be in everlasting remembrance.

Proverbs 22: 9

He that hath a bountiful eye shall be blessed; for he giveth of his bread to the poor.

1 Timothy 6: 17
Charge them that are rich in this world, that they be not highminded, nor trust in uncertain riches, but in the living God, who giveth us richly all things to enjoy;

Proverbs 28: 27
He that giveth unto the poor shall not lack: but he that hideth his eyes shall have many a curse.

Isaiah 58: 6 - 8
Is not this the fast that I have chosen? to loose the bands of wickedness, to undo the heavy burdens, and to let the oppressed go free, and that ye break every yoke? Is it not to deal thy bread to the hungry, and that thou bring the poor that are cast out to thy house? when thou seest the naked, that thou cover him; and that thou hide not thyself from thine own flesh? Then shall thy light break forth as the morning, and thine health shall spring forth speedily: and thy righteousness shall go before thee; the glory of the Lord shall be thy rereward.

Mark 9: 41
For whosoever shall give you a cup of water to drink in my name, because ye belong to Christ, verily I say unto you, he shall not lose his reward.

His Presence

God is as close as the very air we breathe. We cannot experience a human emotion that God is outside of. In ways that are often incomprehensible at the time, God is present at the point of our greatest sense of brokenness and abandonment. The theology of the profound love of God understands that God has entered the drama and trauma of our lives and even screams with us in despair. Jesus, who was in the beginning with God, and who is indeed God, promises never to leave or forsake us. The profound love of God moved Him to take on flesh and hang on a cross where He screamed in agony, "My God, my God, why . . ." (Matt. 27:46).

— C. Swafford Harris

Matthew 18: 20
For where two or three are gathered together in my name, there am I in the midst of them.

Acts 17: 24 - 28
God that made the world and all things therein, seeing that he is Lord of heaven and earth, dwelleth not in temples made with hands; Neither is worshipped with men's hands, as though he needed any thing, seeing he giveth to all life, and breath, and all things; And hath made of one blood all nations of men for to dwell on all the face of the earth, and hath determined the times before appointed, and the bounds of their habitation; That they should seek the Lord, if haply they might feel after him, and find him, though he be not far from every one of us: For in him we live, and move, and have our being; as certain also of your own poets have said, For we are also his offspring.

Psalm 23: 4
Yea, though I walk through the valley of the shadow of death, I will fear no evil: for thou art with me; thy rod and thy staff they comfort me.

Deuteronomy 31: 6
Be strong and of a good courage, fear not, nor be afraid of them: for the Lord thy God, he it is that doth go with thee; he will not fail thee, nor forsake thee.

Matthew 28: 20
Teaching them to observe all things whatsoever I have commanded you: and, lo, I am with you alway, even unto the end of the world. Amen.

Psalm 145: 18
The Lord is nigh unto all them that call upon him, to all that call upon him in truth.

John 14: 16 - 17
And I will pray the Father, and he shall give you another Comforter, that he may abide with you for ever; Even the Spirit of truth; whom the world cannot receive, because it seeth him not, neither knoweth him: but ye know him; for he dwelleth with you, and shall be in you.

Psalm 139: 1, 9 - 10
O Lord, thou hast searched me, and known me. If I take the wings of the morning, and dwell in the uttermost parts of the sea; Even there shall thy hand lead me, and thy right hand shall hold me.

Isaiah 43: 2 - 3
When thou passest through the waters, I will be with thee; and through the rivers, they shall not overflow thee: when thou walkest through the fire, thou shalt not be burned; neither shall the flame kindle upon thee. For I am the Lord thy God, the Holy One of Israel, thy Saviour: I gave Egypt for thy ransom, Ethiopia and Seba for thee.

Exodus 33: 14
And he said, My presence shall go with thee, and I will give thee rest.

Romans 8: 11
But if the Spirit of him that raised up Jesus from the dead dwell in you, he that raised up Christ from the dead shall also quicken your mortal bodies by his Spirit that dwelleth in you.

His Word

John 1: 1 - 4
In the beginning was the Word, and the Word was with God, and the Word was God.
The same was in the beginning with God. All things were made by him; and without him was not any thing made that was made. In him was life; and the life was the light of men.

Matthew 4: 4
But he answered and said, It is written, Man shall not live by bread alone, but by every word that proceedeth out of the mouth of God

Luke 11: 28
But he said, Yea rather, blessed are they that hear the word of God, and keep it.

Psalm 119: 11
Thy word have I hid in mine heart, that I might not sin against thee.

Jeremiah 15: 16
Thy words were found, and I did eat them; and thy word was unto me the joy and rejoicing of mine heart: for I am called by thy name, O Lord God of hosts.

Psalm 119: 165
Great peace have they which love thy law: and nothing shall offend them.

2 Timothy 2: 15
Study to shew thyself approved unto God, a workman that needeth not to be ashamed, rightly dividing the word of truth.

Psalm 119: 105
Thy word is a lamp unto my feet, and a light unto my path.

2 Timothy 3: 16 - 17
All scripture is given by inspiration of God, and is profitable for doctrine, for reproof, for correction, for instruction in righteousness: That the man of God may be perfect, throughly furnished unto all good works.

Romans 15: 4
Yea, thou castest off fear, and restrainest prayer before God.

Psalm 119: 73
Thy hands have made me and fashioned me:
give me understanding, that I may learn thy commandments.

Psalm 119: 97 - 99
O how love I thy law! it is my meditation all the day. Thou through thy commandments hast made me wiser than mine enemies: for they are ever with me. I have more understanding than all my teachers: for thy testimonies are my meditation.

Colossians 3: 16
Let the word of Christ dwell in you richly in all wisdom; teaching and admonishing one another in psalms and hymns and spiritual songs, singing with grace in your hearts to the Lord.

Psalm 119: 129 -130
Thy testimonies are wonderful: therefore doth my soul keep them. The entrance of thy words giveth light; it giveth understanding unto the simple.

Hebrews 4: 12
For the word of God is quick, and powerful, and sharper than any two-edged sword, piercing even to the dividing asunder of soul and spirit, and of the joints and marrow, and is a discerner of the thoughts and intents of the heart.

Mark 13: 31
Heaven and earth shall pass away: but my words shall not pass away.

Grace

"I'm fulfilled in what I do. I never thought that a lot of money or fine clothes--the finer things of life--would make you happy. My concept of happiness is to be filled in a spiritual sense."

— Coretta Scott King,
wife of Martin Luther King Jr.

Graciousness is not a forced action but one that is done with what may appear as effortless skill. A woman who is gracious has the capacity to respond in joy to the various situations of life.

— C. Williams-Neal

Titus 3: 4 -7
But after that the kindness and love of God our Saviour toward man appeared, Not by works of righteousness which we have done, but according to his mercy he saved us, by the washing of regeneration, and renewing of the

Holy Ghost; Which he shed on us abundantly through Jesus Christ our Saviour; That being justified by his grace, we should be made heirs according to the hope of eternal life.

Ephesians 4: 17
This I say therefore, and testify in the Lord, that ye henceforth walk not as other Gentiles walk, in the vanity of their mind,

2 Peter 1: 2
Grace and peace be multiplied unto you through the knowledge of God, and of Jesus our Lord,

2 Corinthians 8: 9
For ye know the grace of our Lord Jesus Christ, that, though he was rich, yet for your sakes he became poor, that ye through his poverty might be rich.

1 Peter 5: 10
But the God of all grace, who hath called us unto his eternal glory by Christ Jesus, after that ye have suffered a while, make you perfect, stablish, strengthen, settle you.

Ephesians 2: 8 - 9
For by grace are ye saved through faith; and that not of yourselves: it is the gift of God: Not of works, lest any man should boast.

John 1: 16 - 18
And of his fulness have all we received, and grace for grace. For the law was given by Moses, but grace and truth came by Jesus Christ. No man hath seen God at any time; the only begotten Son, which is in the bosom of the Father, he hath declared him.

Romans 3: 23 - 26

For all have sinned, and come short of the glory of God; Being justified freely by his grace through the redemption that is in Christ Jesus: Whom God hath set forth to be a propitiation through faith in his blood, to declare his righteousness for the remission of sins that are past, through the forbearance of God; To declare, I say, at this time his righteousness: that he might be just, and the justifier of him which believeth in Jesus.

2 Corinthians 12: 9

And he said unto me, My grace is sufficient for thee: for my strength is made perfect in weakness. Most gladly therefore will I rather glory in my infirmities, that the power of Christ may rest upon me.

1 Corinthians 1: 4 - 5

I thank my God always on your behalf, for the grace of God which is given you by Jesus Christ; That in every thing ye are enriched by him, in all utterance, and in all knowledge;

Ephesians 2: 4 - 7

But God, who is rich in mercy, for his great love wherewith he loved us, Even when we were dead in sins, hath quickened us together with Christ, (by grace ye are saved;) And hath raised us up together, and made us sit together in heavenly places in Christ Jesus: That in the ages to come he might shew the exceeding riches of his grace in his kindness toward us through Christ Jesus.

Guidance

"You will be wounded many times in your life. You'll make mistakes. Some people will call them failures but I have learned that failure is really God's way of saying, "Excuse me, you're moving in the wrong direction." It's just an experience, just an experience."

– Oprah Winfrey

"Success doesn't come to you...you go to it."

– Marva Collins

Proverbs 3: 5 - 6
Trust in the Lord with all thine heart; and lean not unto thine own understanding. In all thy ways acknowledge him, and he shall direct thy paths.

Isaiah 58: 11
And the Lord shall guide thee continually, and satisfy thy soul in drought, and make fat thy bones: and thou shalt be like a watered garden, and like a spring of water, whose waters fail not.

John 16: 13
Howbeit when he, the Spirit of truth, is come, he will guide you into all truth: for he shall not speak of himself; but whatsoever he shall hear, that shall he speak: and he will shew you things to come.

Jeremiah 29: 11
For I know the thoughts that I think toward you, saith the Lord, thoughts of peace, and not of evil, to give you an expected end.

Psalm 31: 3
For thou art my rock and my fortress; therefore for thy name's sake lead me, and guide me.

Psalm 23: 1 - 3
The Lord is my shepherd; I shall not want. He maketh me to lie down in green pastures: he leadeth me beside the still waters. He restoreth my soul: he leadeth me in the paths of righteousness for his name's sake.

Proverbs 6: 20 - 22
My son, keep thy father's commandment, and forsake not the law of thy mother: Bind them continually upon thine heart, and tie them about thy neck. When thou goest, it shall lead thee; when thou sleepest, it shall keep thee; and when thou awakest, it shall talk with thee.

Psalm 32: 8
I will instruct thee and teach thee in the way which thou shalt go: I will guide thee with mine eye.

Psalm 37: 23
The steps of a good man are ordered by the Lord: and he delighteth in his way.

Isaiah 48: 17
Thus saith the Lord, thy Redeemer, the Holy One of Israel; I am the Lord thy God which teacheth thee to profit, which leadeth thee by the way that thou shouldest go.

Proverbs 4: 10 - 13
Hear, O my son, and receive my sayings; and the years of thy life shall be many. I have taught thee in the way of wisdom; I have led thee in right paths. When thou goest, thy steps shall not be straitened; and when thou runnest, thou shalt not stumble. Take fast hold of instruction; let her not go: keep her; for she is thy life.

Ecclesiastes 8: 5
Whoso keepeth the commandment shall feel no evil thing: and a wise man's heart discerneth both time and judgment.

Psalm 139: 1, 9 - 10
O Lord, thou hast searched me, and known me. If I take the wings of the morning, and dwell in the uttermost parts of the sea; Even there shall thy hand lead me, and thy right hand shall hold me.

Health and Healing

New day, new Blessing.
Don't let yesterdays failures ruin the beauty of today,
because each day has its own promise of love,
joy, and forgiveness. Good Morning

—Onuh Justus Izuchukwu

Exodus 23: 25 - 26
And ye shall serve the Lord your God, and he shall bless thy bread, and thy water; and I will take sickness away from the midst of thee. There shall nothing cast their young, nor be barren, in thy land: the number of thy days I will fulfil.

Psalm 34: 18

The Lord is nigh unto them that are of a broken heart; and saveth such as be of a contrite spirit.

James 5 : 14 - 15

Is any sick among you? let him call for the elders of the church; and let them pray over him, anointing him with oil in the name of the Lord: And the prayer of faith shall save the sick, and the Lord shall raise him up; and if he have committed sins, they shall be forgiven him.

Isaiah 53: 5

But he was wounded for our transgressions, he was bruised for our iniquities: the chastisement of our peace was upon him; and with his stripes we are healed.

Jeremiah 33: 6

Behold, I will bring it health and cure, and I will cure them, and will reveal unto them the abundance of peace and truth.

Malachi 4: 2

But unto you that fear my name shall the Sun of righteousness arise with healing in his wings; and ye shall go forth, and grow up as calves of the stall.

Psalm 103: 2 - 3

Bless the Lord, O my soul, and forget not all his benefits: Who forgiveth all thine iniquities; who healeth all thy diseases;

1 Peter 2: 21, 24

For even hereunto were ye called: because Christ also suffered for us, leaving us an example, that ye should follow his steps: For even hereunto were ye called: because Christ also suffered for us, leaving us an example, that ye should follow his steps:

Jeremiah 17: 14

Heal me, O Lord, and I shall be healed; save me, and I shall be saved: for thou art my praise.

Psalm 147: 3

He healeth the broken in heart, and bindeth up their wounds.

Jeremiah 30: 17

For I will restore health unto thee, and I will heal thee of thy wounds, saith the Lord; because they called thee an Outcast, saying, This is Zion, whom no man seeketh after.

Psalm 30: 1 - 2

I will extol thee, O Lord; for thou hast lifted me up, and hast not made my foes to rejoice over me. O Lord my God, I cried unto thee, and thou hast healed me.

2 Chronicles 7: 14

If my people, which are called by my name, shall humble themselves, and pray, and seek my face, and turn from their wicked ways; then will I hear from heaven, and will forgive their sin, and will heal their land.

Psalm 43: 5

Why art thou cast down, O my soul? and why art thou disquieted within me? hope in God: for I shall yet praise him, who is the health of my countenance, and my God.

James 5: 16

Confess your faults one to another, and pray one for another, that ye may be healed. The effectual fervent prayer of a righteous man availeth much.

Heaven

*When I stand before God at the end of my life,
I would hope that I would not have a single bit
of talent left, and could say, "
I used everything You gave me".*

— Erma Bombeck - comedian

John 14: 2 - 3
In my Father's house are many mansions: if it were not so,
I would have told you. I go to prepare a place for you. And
if I go and prepare a place for you, I will come again, and
receive you unto myself; that where I am, there ye may be
also.

Matthew 18: 18
Verily I say unto you, Whatsoever ye shall bind on earth
shall be bound in heaven: and whatsoever ye shall loose
on earth shall be loosed in heaven.

2 Corinthians 5: 1

For we know that if our earthly house of this tabernacle were dissolved, we have a building of God, an house not made with hands, eternal in the heavens.

Luke 17: 21

Neither shall they say, Lo here! or, lo there! for, behold, the kingdom of God is within you.

Romans 14: 17

For the kingdom of God is not meat and drink; but righteousness, and peace, and joy in the Holy Ghost.

1 Peter 1: 3 - 5

Blessed be the God and Father of our Lord Jesus Christ, which according to his abundant mercy hath begotten us again unto a lively hope by the resurrection of Jesus Christ from the dead, To an inheritance incorruptible, and undefiled, and that fadeth not away, reserved in heaven for you, Who are kept by the power of God through faith unto salvation ready to be revealed in the last time.

Matthew 6: 31 - 33

Therefore take no thought, saying, What shall we eat? or, What shall we drink? or, Wherewithal shall we be clothed? (For after all these things do the Gentiles seek:) for your heavenly Father knoweth that ye have need of all these things. But seek ye first the kingdom of God, and his righteousness; and all these things shall be added unto you.

Hebrews 12: 28
Wherefore we receiving a kingdom which cannot be moved, let us have grace, whereby we may serve God acceptably with reverence and godly fear:

1 Chronicles 29: 11
Thine, O Lord, is the greatness, and the power, and the glory, and the victory, and the majesty: for all that is in the heaven and in the earth is thine; thine is the kingdom, O Lord, and thou art exalted as head above all.

Luke 10: 20
Notwithstanding in this rejoice not, that the spirits are subject unto you; but rather rejoice, because your names are written in heaven.

2 Timothy 4: 18
And the Lord shall deliver me from every evil work, and will preserve me unto his heavenly kingdom: to whom be glory for ever and ever. Amen.

James 2: 5
Hearken, my beloved brethren, Hath not God chosen the poor of this world rich in faith, and heirs of the kingdom which he hath promised to them that love him?

Colossians 1: 12 - 14
Giving thanks unto the Father, which hath made us meet to be partakers of the inheritance of the saints in light: Who hath delivered us from the power of darkness, and hath translated us into the kingdom of his dear Son: In whom we have redemption through his blood, even the forgiveness of sins:

Honesty

"Keep working hard and you can get anything that you want. If God gave you the talent, you should go for it. But don't think it's going to be easy. It's hard!"

– Aaliyah

Psalm 25: 4 - 5
Shew me thy ways, O Lord; teach me thy paths. Lead me in thy truth, and teach me: for thou art the God of my salvation; on thee do I wait all the day.

Psalm 41: 12
And as for me, thou upholdest me in mine integrity, and settest me before thy face for ever.

1 Chronicles 29: 17

I know also, my God, that thou triest the heart, and hast pleasure in uprightness. As for me, in the uprightness of mine heart I have willingly offered all these things: and now have I seen with joy thy people, which are present here, to offer willingly unto thee.

Philippians 4: 8 - 9

Finally, brethren, whatsoever things are true, whatsoever things are honest, whatsoever things are just, whatsoever things are pure, whatsoever things are lovely, whatsoever things are of good report; if there be any virtue, and if there be any praise, think on these things. Those things, which ye have both learned, and received, and heard, and seen in me, do: and the God of peace shall be with you.

Proverbs 20: 7

The just man walketh in his integrity: his children are blessed after him.

Psalm 145: 18

The Lord is nigh unto all them that call upon him, to all that call upon him in truth.

Luke 8: 4 - 5, 8, 11, 15

And when much people were gathered together, and were come to him out of every city, he spake by a parable: A sower went out to sow his seed: and as he sowed, some fell by the way side; and it was trodden down, and the fowls of the air devoured it. Now the parable is this: The seed is the word of God. And other fell on good ground, and sprang up, and bare fruit an hundredfold. And when he had said these things, he cried, He that hath ears to hear, let him hear. But that on the good ground are they, which in an honest and good heart, having heard the word, keep it, and bring forth fruit with patience.

Proverbs 2: 7
He layeth up sound wisdom for the righteous: he is a buckler to them that walk uprightly.

Psalm 26: 1
Judge me, O Lord; for I have walked in mine integrity: I have trusted also in the Lord; therefore I shall not slide.

Psalm 40: 11
Withhold not thou thy tender mercies from me, O Lord: let thy lovingkindness and thy truth continually preserve me.

Proverbs 10: 31
The mouth of the just bringeth forth wisdom: but the froward tongue shall be cut out.

Psalm 25: 20 - 21
O keep my soul, and deliver me: let me not be ashamed; for I put my trust in thee. Let integrity and uprightness preserve me; for I wait on thee.

Proverbs 10: 9
He lieth in wait secretly as a lion in his den: he lieth in wait to catch the poor: he doth catch the poor, when he draweth him into his net.

Proverbs 12: 22
Lying lips are abomination to the Lord: but they that deal truly are his delight.

Psalm 51: 6
Behold, thou desirest truth in the inward parts: and in the hidden part thou shalt make me to know wisdom.

Proverbs 11: 3
The integrity of the upright shall guide them: but the perverseness of transgressors shall destroy them.

Proverbs 24: 26
Every man shall kiss his lips that giveth a right answer.

Psalm 7: 8 - 10
So shall the congregation of the people compass thee about: for their sakes therefore return thou on high. The Lord shall judge the people: judge me, O Lord, according to my righteousness, and according to mine integrity that is in me.

Hope

*"We will be ourselves and free,
or die in the attempt.
Harriet Tubman was not our great-grandmother
for nothing."*

Romans 15: 13
Now the God of hope fill you with all joy and peace in believing, that ye may abound in hope, through the power of the Holy Ghost.

Psalm 31: 24
Be of good courage, and he shall strengthen your heart, all ye that hope in the Lord.

Psalm 146: 5 - 6
Happy is he that hath the God of Jacob for his help, whose hope is in the Lord his God: Which made heaven, and earth, the sea, and all that therein is: which keepeth truth for ever:

Lamentations 3: 21 - 24

This I recall to my mind, therefore have I hope. It is of the Lord's mercies that we are not consumed, because his compassions fail not. They are new every morning: great is thy faithfulness. The Lord is my portion, saith my soul; therefore will I hope in him.

Psalm 33: 18

Behold, the eye of the Lord is upon them that fear him, upon them that hope in his mercy;

Romans 5: 1 - 5

Therefore being justified by faith, we have peace with God through our Lord Jesus Christ: By whom also we have access by faith into this grace wherein we stand, and rejoice in hope of the glory of God. And not only so, but we glory in tribulations also: knowing that tribulation worketh patience; And patience, experience; and experience, hope: And hope maketh not ashamed; because the love of God is shed abroad in our hearts by the Holy Ghost which is given unto us.

Psalm 43: 5

Why art thou cast down, O my soul? and why art thou disquieted within me? hope in God: for I shall yet praise him, who is the health of my countenance, and my God.

Romans 15: 4

For whatsoever things were written aforetime were written for our learning, that we through patience and comfort of the scriptures might have hope.

Titus 2 11- 13
For the grace of God that bringeth salvation hath appeared to all men, Teaching us that, denying ungodliness and worldly lusts, we should live soberly, righteously, and godly, in this present world; Looking for that blessed hope, and the glorious appearing of the great God and our Saviour Jesus Christ;

Psalm 147: 11
The Lord taketh pleasure in them that fear him, in those that hope in his mercy.

Lamentations 3: 26
It is good that a man should both hope and quietly wait for the salvation of the Lord.

Micah 7: 18 - 19
Who is a God like unto thee, that pardoneth iniquity, and passeth by the transgression of the remnant of his heritage? he retaineth not his anger for ever, because he delighteth in mercy. He will turn again, he will have compassion upon us; he will subdue our iniquities; and thou wilt cast all their sins into the depths of the sea.

Humility

"African women in general need to know that it's OK for them to be the way they are – to see the way they are as a strength, and to be liberated from fear and from silence."

– Wangari Maathai

Proverbs 22: 4
By humility and the fear of the Lord are riches, and honour, and life.

Psalm 25: 9
The meek will he guide in judgment: and the meek will he teach his way.

Matthew 18: 2, 4
And Jesus called a little child unto him, and set him in the midst of them, Whosoever therefore shall humble himself as this little child, the same is greatest in the kingdom of heaven.

Psalm 147: 5 - 6
Great is our Lord, and of great power: his understanding is infinite. The Lord lifteth up the meek: he casteth the wicked down to the ground.

Proverbs 15: 33
The fear of the Lord is the instruction of wisdom; and before honour is humility.

James 4: 6, 10
But he giveth more grace. Wherefore he saith, God resisteth the proud, but giveth grace unto the humble. Humble yourselves in the sight of the Lord, and he shall lift you up.

Proverbs 29: 23
A man's pride shall bring him low: but honour shall uphold the humble in spirit.

Luke 1: 51 - 53
He hath shewed strength with his arm; he hath scattered the proud in the imagination of their hearts. He hath put down the mighty from their seats, and exalted them of low degree. He hath filled the hungry with good things; and the rich he hath sent empty away.

Psalm 149: 4
For the Lord taketh plesure in his people: he will beautify the meek with salvation.

1 Peter 5: 5 - 7
Likewise, ye younger, submit yourselves unto the elder. Yea, all of you be subject one to another, and be clothed with humility:

for God resisteth the proud, and giveth grace to the humble. Humble yourselves therefore under the mighty hand of God, that he may exalt you in due time: Casting all your care upon him; for he careth for you.

Luke 18: 14
I tell you, this man went down to his house justified rather than the other: for every one that exalteth himself shall be abased; and he that humbleth himself shall be exalted.

Proverbs 16: 19
Better it is to be of an humble spirit with the lowly, than to divide the spoil with the proud.

Proverbs 11: 2
When pride cometh, then cometh shame: but with the lowly is wisdom.

Isaiah 57: 15
For thus saith the high and lofty One that inhabiteth eternity, whose name is Holy; I dwell in the high and holy place, with him also that is of a contrite and humble spirit, to revive the spirit of the humble, and to revive the heart of the contrite ones.

Matthew 5: 3, 5
Blessed are the poor in spirit: for theirs is the kingdom of heaven. Blessed are the meek: for they shall inherit the earth.

Micah 6: 8
He hath shewed thee, O man, what is good; and what doth the Lord require of thee, but to do justly, and to love mercy, and to walk humbly with thy God?

Proverbs 10: 27
The fear of the Lord prolongeth days: but the years of the wicked shall be shortened.

Psalm 45: 4
And in thy majesty ride prosperously because of truth and meekness and righteousness; and thy right hand shall teach thee terrible things.

Psalm 37: 11
But the meek shall inherit the earth; and shall delight themselves in the abundance of peace.

Joy

"Once we recognize what it is we are feeling, once we recognize we can feel deeply, love deeply, can feel joy, then we will demand that all parts of our lives produce that kind of joy."

– Audre Lorde

John 16: 20, 22
Verily, verily, I say unto you, That ye shall weep and lament, but the world shall rejoice: and ye shall be sorrowful, but your sorrow shall be turned into joy. And ye now therefore have sorrow: but I will see you again, and your heart shall rejoice, and your joy no man taketh from you.

Psalm 126: 5 - 6
They that sow in tears shall reap in joy. He that goeth forth and weepeth, bearing precious seed, shall doubtless come again with rejoicing, bringing his sheaves with him.

Psalm 97: 11
Light is sown for the righteous, and gladness for the upright in heart.

Deuteronomy 16: 15
Seven days shalt thou keep a solemn feast unto the Lord thy God in the place which the Lord shall choose: because the Lord thy God shall bless thee in all thine increase, and in all the works of thine hands, therefore thou shalt surely rejoice.

Isaiah 61: 10
I will greatly rejoice in the Lord, my soul shall be joyful in my God; for he hath clothed me with the garments of salvation, he hath covered me with the robe of righteousness, as a bridegroom decketh himself with ornaments, and as a bride adorneth herself with her jewels.

Psalm 128: 1 - 2
Blessed is every one that feareth the Lord; that walketh in his ways. For thou shalt eat the labour of thine hands: happy shalt thou be, and it shall be well with thee.

Proverbs 15: 23
A man hath joy by the answer of his mouth: and a word spoken in due season, how good is it!

John 16: 24
Hitherto have ye asked nothing in my name: ask, and ye shall receive, that your joy may be full.

1 Peter 3: 14
But and if ye suffer for righteousness' sake, happy are ye: and be not afraid of their terror, neither be troubled;

Ecclesiastes 2: 26

For God giveth to a man that is good in his sight wisdom, and knowledge, and joy: but to the sinner he giveth travail, to gather and to heap up, that he may give to him that is good before God. This also is vanity and vexation of spirit.

Proverbs 14: 21

He that despiseth his neighbour sinneth: but he that hath mercy on the poor, happy is he.

Psalm 30: 11

Thou hast turned for me my mourning into dancing: thou hast put off my sackcloth, and girded me with gladness;

Psalm 16: 11

Thou wilt shew me the path of life: in thy presence is fulness of joy; at thy right hand there are pleasures for evermore.

Psalm 92: 4

For thou, Lord, hast made me glad through thy work: I will triumph in the works of thy hands.

Acts 2: 28

Thou hast made known to me the ways of life; thou shalt make me full of joy with thy countenance.

Psalm 144: 15

Happy is that people, that is in such a case: yea, happy is that people, whose God is the Lord.

Proverbs 29: 18

Where there is no vision, the people perish: but he that keepeth the law, happy is he.

Proverbs 3: 13
Happy is the man that findeth wisdom, and the man that getteth understanding.

Isaiah 25: 10
For in this mountain shall the hand of the Lord rest, and Moab shall be trodden down under him, even as straw is trodden down for the dunghill.

Psalm 16: 8 - 9
I have set the Lord always before me: because he is at my right hand, I shall not be moved. Therefore my heart is glad, and my glory rejoiceth: my flesh also shall rest in hope.

Isaiah 12: 2 - 6
Behold, God is my salvation; I will trust, and not be afraid: for the Lord Jehovah is my strength and my song; he also is become my salvation. Therefore with joy shall ye draw water out of the wells of salvation. And in that day shall ye say, Praise the Lord, call upon his name, declare his doings among the people, make mention that his name is exalted. Sing unto the Lord; for he hath done excellent things: this is known in all the earth.
Cry out and shout, thou inhabitant of Zion: for great is the Holy One of Israel in the midst of thee.

Hebrews 1: 9
Thou hast loved righteousness, and hated iniquity; therefore God, even thy God, hath anointed thee with the oil of gladness above thy fellows.

Romans 15: 13
Now the God of hope fill you with all joy and peace in believing, that ye may abound in hope, through the power of the Holy Ghost.

Psalm 47: 1 - 2
O clap your hands, all ye people; shout unto God with the voice of triumph. For the Lord most high is terrible; he is a great King over all the earth.

Isaiah 65: 17 - 19
For, behold, I create new heavens and a new earth: and the former shall not be remembered, nor come into mind. But be ye glad and rejoice for ever in that which I create: for, behold, I create Jerusalem a rejoicing, and her people a joy. And I will rejoice in Jerusalem, and joy in my people: and the voice of weeping shall be no more heard in her, nor the voice of crying.

Kindness

"We never know how high we are
Till we are called to rise;
And then, if we are true to plan,
Our statures touch the skies."

— Emily Dickinson, American poet

We live in a world where we are taught to look out
for number one, to take care of our own, and to let
others fend for themselves. But God calls us to another
standard. We are told to maintain good works, to show
a pattern of good works, and to be zealous of good
works. Many persons will only see the goodness of God
as they witness that goodness in us.

—C. Belt

Jeremiah 9: 24
But let him that glorieth glory in this, that he understandeth
and knoweth me, that I am the Lord which exercise loving
kindness, judgment, and righteousness, in the earth: for
in these things I delight, saith the Lord.

Psalm 117: 1 - 2

O praise the Lord, all ye nations: praise him, all ye people. For his merciful kindness is great toward us: and the truth of the Lord endureth for ever. Praise ye the Lord.

Galatians 6: 10

As we have therefore opportunity, let us do good unto all men, especially unto them who are of the household of faith.

Micah 7: 19

He will turn again, he will have compassion upon us; he will subdue our iniquities; and thou wilt cast all their sins into the depths of the sea.

Psalm 111: 4

He hath made his wonderful works to be remembered: the Lord is gracious and full of compassion.

James 5: 11

Behold, we count them happy which endure. Ye have heard of the patience of Job, and have seen the end of the Lord; that the Lord is very pitiful, and of tender mercy.

Nehemiah 9: 17

And refused to obey, neither were mindful of thy wonders that thou didst among them; but hardened their necks, and in their rebellion appointed a captain to return to their bondage: but thou art a God ready to pardon, gracious and merciful, slow to anger, and of great kindness, and forsookest them not.

Proverbs 31: 10. 26

Who can find a virtuous woman? for her price is far above rubies. She openeth her mouth with wisdom; and in her tongue is the law of kindness.

Psalm 119: 76 - 77
Let, I pray thee, thy merciful kindness be for my comfort, according to thy word unto thy servant. Let thy tender mercies come unto me, that I may live: for thy law is my delight.

Psalm 31: 21
Blessed be the Lord: for he hath shewed me his marvelous kindness in a strong city.

Isaiah 54: 10
For the mountains shall depart, and the hills be removed; but my kindness shall not depart from thee, neither shall the covenant of my peace be removed, saith the Lord that hath mercy on thee.

Psalm 112: 4
Unto the upright there ariseth light in the darkness: he is gracious, and full of compassion, and righteous.

Psalm 119: 156
Great are thy tender mercies, O Lord: quicken me according to thy judgments.

2 Chronicles 30: 9
For if ye turn again unto the Lord, your brethren and your children shall find compassion before them that lead them captive, so that they shall come again into this land: for the Lord your God is gracious and merciful, and will not turn away his face from you, if ye return unto him.

Psalm 86: 15
But thou, O Lord, art a God full of compassion, and gracious, longsuffering, and plenteous in mercy and truth.

Psalm 145: 9
The Lord is good to all: and his tender mercies are over all his works.

Love

"The times may have changed, but the people are still the same. We're still looking for love, and that will always be our struggle as human beings."

– Halle Berry

John 14: 21
He that hath my commandments, and keepeth them, he it is that loveth me: and he that loveth me shall be loved of my Father, and I will love him, and will manifest myself to him.

Ephesians 2: 4 - 6
But God, who is rich in mercy, for his great love wherewith he loved us, Even when we were dead in sins, hath quickened us together with Christ, (by grace ye are saved;) And hath raised us up together, and made us sit together in heavenly places in Christ Jesus:

Matthew 5: 44 - 45
But I say unto you, Love your enemies, bless them that curse you, do good to them that hate you, and pray for them which despitefully use you, and persecute you; That ye may be the children of your Father which is in heaven: for he maketh his sun to rise on the evil and on the good, and sendeth rain on the just and on the unjust.

Colossians 3: 12 - 14

Put on therefore, as the elect of God, holy and beloved, bowels of mercies, kindness, humbleness of mind, meekness, longsuffering; Forbearing one another, and forgiving one another, if any man have a quarrel against any: even as Christ forgave you, so also do ye. And above all these things put on charity, which is the bond of perfectness.

1 Corinthians 13: 4 - 8

Charity suffereth long, and is kind; charity envieth not; charity vaunteth not itself, is not puffed up, Doth not behave itself unseemly, seeketh not her own, is not easily provoked, thinketh no evil; Rejoiceth not in iniquity, but rejoiceth in the truth; Beareth all things, believeth all things, hopeth all things, endureth all things. Charity never faileth: but whether there be prophecies, they shall fail; whether there be tongues, they shall cease; whether there be knowledge, it shall vanish away.

Romans 8: 38 - 39

For I am persuaded, that neither death, nor life, nor angels, nor principalities, nor powers, nor things present, nor things to come, Nor height, nor depth, nor any other creature, shall be able to separate us from the love of God, which is in Christ Jesus our Lord.

1 Corinthians 13: 13

And now abideth faith, hope, charity, these three; but the greatest of these is charity.

1 John 4: 7

Beloved, let us love one another: for love is of God; and every one that loveth is born of God, and knoweth God.

John 14: 23

Jesus answered and said unto him, If a man love me, he will keep my words: and my Father will love him, and we will come unto him, and make our abode with him.

1 John 4: 18

There is no fear in love; but perfect love casteth out fear: because fear hath torment. He that feareth is not made perfect in love.

Jeremiah 31: 3

The Lord hath appeared of old unto me, saying, Yea, I have loved thee with an everlasting love: therefore with lovingkindness have I drawn thee.

Psalm 146: 8 - 9

The Lord openeth the eyes of the blind: the Lord raiseth them that are bowed down: the Lord loveth the righteous: The Lord preserveth the strangers; he relieveth the fatherless and widow: but the way of the wicked he turneth upside down.

Psalm 143: 7 - 8

Hear me speedily, O Lord: my spirit faileth: hide not thy face from me, lest I be like unto them that go down into the pit. Cause me to hear thy lovingkindness in the morning; for in thee do I trust: cause me to know the way wherein I should walk; for I lift up my soul unto thee.

1 John 4: 12

No man hath seen God at any time. If we love one another, God dwelleth in us, and his love is perfected in us.

Peace

Anybody who believes in something without reservation believes that this thing is right and should be, has the stamina to meet obstacles and overcome them.

— Golda Meir

Many of the things we do on a daily basis have merit and they are indeed worthwhile. But they must be placed in their proper context, however, or peace will continue to evade us. We must come to learn that peace does not come through worldly things or pleasures if it is to last. We must go to its Source.

— C. Richards

Philippians 4: 6 - 7
Be careful for nothing; but in every thing by prayer and supplication with thanksgiving let your requests be made known unto God. And the peace of God, which passeth all understanding, shall keep your hearts and minds through Christ Jesus.

2 Thessalonians 3: 16
Now the Lord of peace himself give you peace always by all means. The Lord be with you all.

Isaiah 26: 3
Thou wilt keep him in perfect peace, whose mind is stayed on thee: because he trusteth in thee.

Matthew 5: 9
Blessed are the peacemakers: for they shall be called the children of God.

Romans 5: 1 - 2
Therefore being justified by faith, we have peace with God through our Lord Jesus Christ: By whom also we have access by faith into this grace wherein we stand, and rejoice in hope of the glory of God.

John 14: 27
Peace I leave with you, my peace I give unto you: not as the world giveth, give I unto you. Let not your heart be troubled, neither let it be afraid.

Romans 10: 15
And how shall they preach, except they be sent? as it is written, How beautiful are the feet of them that preach the gospel of peace, and bring glad tidings of good things!

Romans 14: 17 - 19
For the kingdom of God is not meat and drink; but righteousness, and peace, and joy in the Holy Ghost. For he that in these things serveth Christ is acceptable to God, and approved of men. Let

us therefore follow after the things which make for peace, and things wherewith one may edify another.

Colossians 3:15
And let the peace of God rule in your hearts, to the which also ye are called in one body; and be ye thankful.

Romans 15:13
Now the God of hope fill you with all joy and peace in believing, that ye may abound in hope, through the power of the Holy Ghost.

2 Corinthians 13:11
Finally, brethren, farewell. Be perfect, be of good comfort, be of one mind, live in peace; and the God of love and peace shall be with you.

Romans 8:6
For to be carnally minded is death; but to be spiritually minded is life and peace.

James 3:17 - 18
But the wisdom that is from above is first pure, then peaceable, gentle, and easy to be intreated, full of mercy and good fruits, without partiality, and without hypocrisy. And the fruit of righteousness is sown in peace of them that make peace.

Romans 2:10 - 11
But glory, honour, and peace, to every man that worketh good, to the Jew first, and also to the Gentile: For there is no respect of persons with God.

Proverbs 16: 7
When a man's ways please the Lord, he maketh even his enemies to be at peace with him.

Psalm 119: 165
Great peace have they which love thy law: and nothing shall offend them.

1 Corinthians 14: 33
For God is not the author of confusion, but of peace, as in all churches of the saints.

Isaiah 9: 6
For unto us a child is born, unto us a son is given: and the government shall be upon his shoulder: and his name shall be called Wonderful, Counsellor, The mighty God, The everlasting Father, The Prince of Peace.

Persevering

You can write me down in history with hateful, twisted lies, you can tread me in this very dirt, but still, like dust, I'll rise.

— Maya Angelou, poet, educator

1 Peter 5: 10
But the God of all grace, who hath called us unto his eternal glory by Christ Jesus, after that ye have suffered a while, make you perfect, stablish, strengthen, settle you.

James 1: 12
Blessed is the man that endureth temptation: for when he is tried, he shall receive the crown of life, which the Lord hath promised to them that love him.

Philippians 3: 13 - 14
Brethren, I count not myself to have apprehended: but this one thing I do, forgetting those things which are behind, and reaching forth unto those things which are before, I press toward the mark for the prize of the high calling of God in Christ Jesus.

2 Corinthians 4: 17 - 18
For our light affliction, which is but for a moment, worketh for us a far more exceeding and eternal weight of glory; While we look not at the things which are seen, but at the things which are not seen: for the things which are seen are temporal; but the things which are not seen are eternal.

Hebrews 12: 1 - 2
Wherefore seeing we also are compassed about with so great a cloud of witnesses, let us lay aside every weight, and the sin which doth so easily beset us, and let us run with patience the race that is set before us, Looking unto Jesus the author and finisher of our faith; who for the joy that was set before him endured the cross, despising the shame, and is set down at the right hand of the throne of God.

2 Thessalonians 3: 5
And the Lord direct your hearts into the love of God, and into the patient waiting for Christ.

Romans 2: 7
To them who by patient continuance in well doing seek for glory and honour and immortality, eternal life:

Galatians 6: 9
And let us not be weary in well doing: for in due season we shall reap, if we faint not.

James 1: 2 - 3
My brethren, count it all joy when ye fall into divers temptations; Knowing this, that the trying of your faith worketh patience.

2 Peter 1: 10 - 11
Wherefore the rather, brethren, give diligence to make your calling and election sure: for if ye do these things, ye shall never fall: For so an entrance shall be ministered unto you abundantly into the everlasting kingdom of our Lord and Saviour Jesus Christ.

Psalm 1: 1 - 3
Blessed is the man that walketh not in the counsel of the ungodly, nor standeth in the way of sinners, nor sitteth in the seat of the scornful. But his delight is in the law of the Lord; and in his law doth he meditate day and night. And he shall be like a tree planted by the rivers of water, that bringeth forth his fruit in his season; his leaf also shall not wither; and whatsoever he doeth shall prosper.

James 1: 25
But whoso looketh into the perfect law of liberty, and continueth therein, he being not a forgetful hearer, but a doer of the work, this man shall be blessed in his deed.

Praising & Worshipping

"This is my story, this is my Song,
Praising my Savior, all the day long."

— Fanny Crosby

Psalm 33: 2 - 4
Praise the Lord with harp: sing unto him with the psaltery and an instrument of ten strings. Sing unto him a new song; play skilfully with a loud noise. For the word of the Lord is right; and all his works are done in truth.

Exodus 15: 1 - 2
Then sang Moses and the children of Israel this song unto the Lord, and spake, saying, I will sing unto the Lord, for he hath triumphed gloriously: the horse and his rider hath he thrown into the sea. The Lord is my strength and song, and he is become my salvation: he is my God, and I will prepare him an habitation; my father's God, and I will exalt him.

Psalm 149: 1 - 2
Praise ye the Lord. Sing unto the Lord a new song, and his praise in the congregation of saints. Let Israel rejoice in him that made him: let the children of Zion be joyful in their King.

Psalm 22: 3 - 4
But thou art holy, O thou that inhabitest the praises of Israel. Our fathers trusted in thee: they trusted, and thou didst deliver them.

1 Peter 2: 9, Psalm 149: 5 - 6
Let the saints be joyful in glory: let them sing aloud upon their beds. Let the high praises of God be in their mouth, and a two-edged sword in their hand;

Psalm 33: 1
Rejoice in the Lord, O ye righteous: for praise is comely for the upright.

Psalm 117: 1 - 2
O praise the Lord, all ye nations: praise him, all ye people. For his merciful kindness is great toward us: and the truth of the Lord endureth for ever. Praise ye the Lord.

Isaiah 63: 7 - 8
I will mention the lovingkindnesses of the Lord, and the praises of the Lord, according to all that the Lord hath bestowed on us, and the great goodness toward the house of Israel, which he hath bestowed on them according to his mercies, and according to the multitude of his lovingkindnesses. For he said, Surely they are my people, children that will not lie: so he was their Saviour.

Psalm 30: 1 - 2

I will extol thee, O Lord; for thou hast lifted me up, and hast not made my foes to rejoice over me. O Lord my God, I cried unto thee, and thou hast healed me.

Psalm 95: 6

Honour and majesty are before him: strength and beauty are in his sanctuary.

1 Chronicles 16: 25

For great is the Lord, and greatly to be praised: he also is to be feared above all gods.

Psalm 9: 1 - 2

I will praise thee, O Lord, with my whole heart; I will shew forth all thy marvellous works.
I will be glad and rejoice in thee: I will sing praise to thy name, O thou most High.

Revelation 19: 5 - 6

And a voice came out of the throne, saying, Praise our God, all ye his servants, and ye that fear him, both small and great. And I heard as it were the voice of a great multitude, and as the voice of many waters, and as the voice of mighty thunderings, saying, Alleluia: for the Lord God omnipotent reigneth.

Psalm 149: 3 - 4

Let them praise his name in the dance: let them sing praises unto him with the timbrel and harp. For the Lord taketh pleasure in his people: he will beautify the meek with salvation.

Psalm 29: 1 - 2
Give unto the Lord, O ye mighty, give unto the Lord glory and strength. Give unto the Lord the glory due unto his name; worship the Lord in the beauty of holiness.

John 4: 23
But the hour cometh, and now is, when the true worshippers shall worship the Father in spirit and in truth: for the Father seeketh such to worship him.

Psalm 139: 14
I will praise thee; for I am fearfully and wonderfully made: marvellous are thy works; and that my soul knoweth right well.

Psalm 28: 7
The Lord is my strength and my shield; my heart trusted in him, and I am helped: therefore my heart greatly rejoiceth; and with my song will I praise him.

Psalm 98: 1
O sing unto the Lord a new song; for he hath done marvellous things: his right hand, and his holy arm, hath gotten him the victory.

Psalm 104: 33 - 34
I will sing unto the Lord as long as I live: I will sing praise to my God while I have my being. My meditation of him shall be sweet: I will be glad in the Lord.

Prayer

" God speaks wherever he finds a humble, listening ear,
And the language he uses is kindness.

— Lena Horne, Singer

1 John 5: 14 - 15
And this is the confidence that we have in him, that, if we ask any thing according to his will, he heareth us: And if we know that he hear us, whatsoever we ask, we know that we have the petitions that we desired of him.

Matthew 7: 7 - 8
Ask, and it shall be given you; seek, and ye shall find; knock, and it shall be opened unto you: For every one that asketh receiveth; and he that seeketh findeth; and to him that knocketh it shall be opened

Isaiah 65: 24
And it shall come to pass, that before they call, I will answer; and while they are yet speaking, I will hear.

John 14: 13 - 14
And whatsoever ye shall ask in my name, that will I do, that the Father may be glorified in the Son. If ye shall ask any thing in my name, I will do it.

Psalm 5: 2 - 3
Hearken unto the voice of my cry, my King, and my God: for unto thee will I pray. My voice shalt thou hear in the morning, O Lord; in the morning will I direct my prayer unto thee, and will look up.

Mark 11: 24
Therefore I say unto you, What things soever ye desire, when ye pray, believe that ye receive them, and ye shall have them.

Psalm 55: 16 - 17
As for me, I will call upon God; and the Lord shall save me. Evening, and morning, and at noon, will I pray, and cry aloud: and he shall hear my voice.

Psalm 32: 6
For this shall every one that is godly pray unto thee in a time when thou mayest be found: surely in the floods of great waters they shall not come nigh unto him.

Proverbs 15: 29
The Lord is far from the wicked: but he heareth the prayer of the righteous.

James 5: 16
Confess your faults one to another, and pray one for another, that ye may be healed. The effectual fervent prayer of a righteous man availeth much.

Matthew 21: 21 - 22

Jesus answered and said unto them, Verily I say unto you, If ye have faith, and doubt not, ye shall not only do this which is done to the fig tree, but also if ye shall say unto this mountain, Be thou removed, and be thou cast into the sea; it shall be done. And all things, whatsoever ye shall ask in prayer, believing, ye shall receive.

Proverbs 15: 8

The sacrifice of the wicked is an abomination to the Lord: but the prayer of the upright is his delight.

2 Chronicles 7: 14

If my people, which are called by my name, shall humble themselves, and pray, and seek my face, and turn from their wicked ways; then will I hear from heaven, and will forgive their sin, and will heal their land.

James 5: 15

And the prayer of faith shall save the sick, and the Lord shall raise him up; and if he have committed sins, they shall be forgiven him.

1 Peter 3: 12

For the eyes of the Lord are over the righteous, and his ears are open unto their prayers: but the face of the Lord is against them that do evil.

John 14: 13 - 14

And whatsoever ye shall ask in my name, that will I do, that the Father may be glorified in the Son. If ye shall ask any thing in my name, I will do it.

Romans 8: 33 - 34

Who shall lay any thing to the charge of God's elect? It is God that justifieth. Who is he that condemneth? It is Christ that died, yea rather, that is risen again, who is even at the right hand of God, who also maketh intercession for us.

Psalm 91: 14 - 15

Because he hath set his love upon me, therefore will I deliver him: I will set him on high, because he hath known my name. He shall call upon me, and I will answer him: I will be with him in trouble; I will deliver him, and honour him.

John 16: 23

And in that day ye shall ask me nothing. Verily, verily, I say unto you, Whatsoever ye shall ask the Father in my name, he will give it you.

Psalm 6: 8 - 9

Depart from me, all ye workers of iniquity; for the Lord hath heard the voice of my weeping. The Lord hath heard my supplication; the Lord will receive my prayer.

Romans 8: 26 - 27

Likewise the Spirit also helpeth our infirmities: for we know not what we should pray for as we ought: but the Spirit itself maketh intercession for us with groanings which cannot be uttered. And he that searcheth the hearts knoweth what is the mind of the Spirit, because he maketh intercession for the saints according to the will of God.

Colossians 4: 2
Continue in prayer, and watch in the same with thanksgiving;

Hebrews 7: 25
Wherefore he is able also to save them to the uttermost that come unto God by him, seeing he ever liveth to make intercession for them.

Psalm 102: 17
He will regard the prayer of the destitute, and not despise their prayer.

Mark 11: 25
And when ye stand praying, forgive, if ye have ought against any: that your Father also which is in heaven may forgive you your trespasses.

Protection

"The best protection any woman can have...is courage."

— Elizabeth Cady Stanton,
American abolitionist

Isaiah 41: 10
Fear thou not; for I am with thee: be not dismayed; for I am thy God: I will strengthen thee; yea, I will help thee; yea, I will uphold thee with the right hand of my righteousness.

Psalm 27: 5
For in the time of trouble he shall hide me in his pavilion: in the secret of his tabernacle shall he hide me; he shall set me up upon a rock.

Deuteronomy 33: 12
And of Benjamin he said, The beloved of the Lord shall dwell in safety by him; and the Lord shall cover him all the day long, and he shall dwell between his shoulders.

Proverbs 29: 25

The fear of man bringeth a snare: but whoso putteth his trust in the Lord shall be safe.

Psalm 91: 5 - 7

Thou shalt not be afraid for the terror by night; nor for the arrow that flieth by day; Nor for the pestilence that walketh in darkness; nor for the destruction that wasteth at noonday. A thousand shall fall at thy side, and ten thousand at thy right hand; but it shall not come nigh thee.

Proverbs 2: 7 - 8

He layeth up sound wisdom for the righteous: he is a buckler to them that walk uprightly. He keepeth the paths of judgment, and preserveth the way of his saints.

2 Timothy 4: 18

And the Lord shall deliver me from every evil work, and will preserve me unto his heavenly kingdom: to whom be glory for ever and ever. Amen.

Psalm 55: 22

Cast thy burden upon the Lord, and he shall sustain thee: he shall never suffer the righteous to be moved.

2 Thessalonians 3: 3

We are bound to thank God always for you, brethren, as it is meet, because that your faith groweth exceedingly, and the charity of every one of you all toward each other aboundeth;

1 Peter 3: 13

And who is he that will harm you, if ye be followers of that which is good?

Psalm 121: 5 - 8
The Lord is thy keeper: the Lord is thy shade upon thy right hand. The sun shall not smite thee by day, nor the moon by night. The Lord shall preserve thee from all evil: he shall preserve thy soul. The Lord shall preserve thy going out and thy coming in from this time forth, and even for evermore.

Deuteronomy 33: 27
The eternal God is thy refuge, and underneath are the everlasting arms: and he shall thrust out the enemy from before thee; and shall say, Destroy them.

Psalm 37: 28
For the Lord loveth judgment, and forsaketh not his saints; they are preserved for ever: but the seed of the wicked shall be cut off.

Proverbs 18: 10
The name of the Lord is a strong tower: the righteous runneth into it, and is safe.

Psalm 31: 7 - 8
I will be glad and rejoice in thy mercy: for thou hast considered my trouble; thou hast known my soul in adversities; And hast not shut me up into the hand of the enemy: thou hast set my feet in a large room.

Psalm 91: 2 - 4
I will say of the Lord, He is my refuge and my fortress: my God; in him will I trust. Surely he shall deliver thee from the snare of the fowler, and from the noisome pestilence. He shall cover thee with his feathers, and under his wings shalt thou trust: his truth shall be thy shield and buckler.

Proverbs 30: 5
Every word of God is pure: he is a shield unto them that put their trust in him.

Psalm 17: 8
Keep me as the apple of the eye, hide me under the shadow of thy wings,

Romans 8: 38 - 39
For I am persuaded, that neither death, nor life, nor angels, nor principalities, nor powers, nor things present, nor things to come, Nor height, nor depth, nor any other creature, shall be able to separate us from the love of God, which is in Christ Jesus our Lord.

Psalm 71: 1 - 3
In thee, O Lord, do I put my trust: let me never be put to confusion. Deliver me in thy righteousness, and cause me to escape: incline thine ear unto me, and save me. Be thou my strong habitation, whereunto I may continually resort: thou hast given commandment to save me; for thou art my rock and my fortress.

Proverbs 14: 26
In the fear of the Lord is strong confidence: and his children shall have a place of refuge.

Psalm 34: 7
The angel of the Lord encampeth round about them that fear him, and delivereth them.

Hebrews 13: 6
So that we may boldly say, The Lord is my helper, and I will not fear what man shall do unto me.

Psalm 16: 5
The Lord is the portion of mine inheritance and of my cup: thou maintainest my lot.

Psalm 37: 40
And the Lord shall help them and deliver them: he shall deliver them from the wicked, and save them, because they trust in him.

Providing

"I think the girl who is able to earn her own living and pay her own way should be as happy as anybody on earth. The sense of independence and security is very sweet."

— Susan B. Anthony, American suffragette and advocate of women's rights

Genesis 50: 21
Now therefore fear ye not: I will nourish you, and your little ones. And he comforted them, and spake kindly unto them.

Psalm 111: 5
He hath given meat unto them that fear him: he will ever be mindful of his covenant.

Acts 14: 17
Nevertheless he left not himself without witness, in that he did good, and gave us rain from heaven, and fruitful seasons, filling our hearts with food and gladness.

2 Corinthians 9: 8
And God is able to make all grace abound toward you; that ye, always having all sufficiency in all things, may abound to every good work:

Philippians 4: 19
But my God shall supply all your need according to his riches in glory by Christ Jesus.

Matthew 6: 30 - 32
Wherefore, if God so clothe the grass of the field, which to day is, and to morrow is cast into the oven, shall he not much more clothe you, O ye of little faith? Therefore take no thought, saying, What shall we eat? or, What shall we drink? or, Wherewithal shall we be clothed? (For after all these things do the Gentiles seek:) for your heavenly Father knoweth that ye have need of all these things.

Matthew 7: 9 - 11
Or what man is there of you, whom if his son ask bread, will he give him a stone? Or if he ask a fish, will he give him a serpent? If ye then, being evil, know how to give good gifts unto your children, how much more shall your Father which is in heaven give good things to them that ask him?

Isaiah 58: 11
And the Lord shall guide thee continually, and satisfy thy soul in drought, and make fat thy bones: and thou shalt be like a watered garden, and like a spring of water, whose waters fail not.

Jeremiah 31: 14
And I will satiate the soul of the priests with fatness, and my people shall be satisfied with my goodness, saith the Lord.

2 Corinthians 9: 10 - 11

Now he that ministereth seed to the sower both minister bread for your food, and multiply your seed sown, and increase the fruits of your righteousness;) Being enriched in every thing to all bountifulness, which causeth through us thanksgiving to God.

Psalm 37: 25 - 26

I have been young, and now am old; yet have I not seen the righteous forsaken, nor his seed begging bread. He is ever merciful, and lendeth; and his seed is blessed.

Luke 12: 24, 29 - 31

Consider the ravens: for they neither sow nor reap; which neither have storehouse nor barn; and God feedeth them: how much more are ye better than the fowls? And seek not ye what ye shall eat, or what ye shall drink, neither be ye of doubtful mind. For all these things do the nations of the world seek after: and your Father knoweth that ye have need of these things.

Relationships

Women need the fellowship—the nurturing companionship of other women. Above all things we need the fellowship of God (see Lev. 26:11-13; 1 John 1:3). Friendship between two women is based on love, loyalty, and commitment. An example of a devoted friendship between two women is seen in the New Testament between Elisabeth and Mary (Luke 1:39-56), and in the Old Testament between Ruth and Naomi, a mother-in law/daughter-in-law situation that blossomed into a lifelong friendship. Christian women are encouraged to build lasting friendships that will endure life's challenges.

— A. Howell

John 15: 7
If ye abide in me, and my words abide in you, ye shall ask what ye will, and it shall be done unto you.

Revelation 3: 20
Behold, I stand at the door, and knock: if any man hear my voice, and open the door, I will come in to him, and will sup with him, and he with me.

Proverbs 18: 24
A man that hath friends must shew himself friendly: and there is a friend that sticketh closer than a brother.

Hosea 2: 19 - 20
And I will betroth thee unto me for ever; yea, I will betroth thee unto me in righteousness, and in judgment, and in lovingkindness, and in mercies. I will even betroth thee unto me in faithfulness: and thou shalt know the Lord.

Proverbs 17: 17
A friend loveth at all times, and a brother is born for adversity.

Ecclesiastes 4: 9 - 12
For if they fall, the one will lift up his fellow: but woe to him that is alone when he falleth; for he hath not another to help him up. Again, if two lie together, then they have heat: but how can one be warm alone? And if one prevail against him, two shall withstand him; and a threefold cord is not quickly broken.

Proverbs 27: 6
Faithful are the wounds of a friend; but the kisses of an enemy are deceitful.

2 Corinthians 6: 17 - 18
Wherefore come out from among them, and be ye separate, saith the Lord, and touch not the unclean thing; and I will receive you, And will be a Father unto you, and ye shall be my sons and daughters, saith the Lord Almighty.

Proverbs 27: 17
Iron sharpeneth iron; so a man sharpeneth the countenance of his friend.

John 15: 13 - 15
Greater love hath no man than this, that a man lay down his life for his friends. Ye are my friends, if ye do whatsoever I command you. Henceforth I call you not servants; for the servant knoweth not what his lord doeth: but I have called you friends; for all things that I have heard of my Father I have made known unto you.

Psalm 27: 10
When my father and my mother forsake me, then the Lord will take me up.

Matthew 28: 20
Teaching them to observe all things whatsoever I have commanded you: and, lo, I am with you alway, even unto the end of the world. Amen.

Proverbs 13: 20
He that walketh with wise men shall be wise: but a companion of fools shall be destroyed.

Romans 8: 32
He that spared not his own Son, but delivered him up for us all, how shall he not with him also freely give us all things?

1 John 1: 7
But if we walk in the light, as he is in the light, we have fellowship one with another, and the blood of Jesus Christ his Son cleanseth us from all sin.

Repentance

Luke 15: 10
Likewise, I say unto you, there is joy in the presence of the angels of God over one sinner that repenteth.

Acts 2: 38
Thou hast made known to me the ways of life; thou shalt make me full of joy with thy countenance.

Luke 15: 7
I say unto you, that likewise joy shall be in heaven over one sinner that repenteth, more than over ninety and nine just persons, which need no repentance.

2 Peter 3: 9
The Lord is not slack concerning his promise, as some men count slackness; but is longsuffering to us-ward, not willing that any should perish, but that all should come to repentance.

Psalm 85: 4 - 5
Turn us, O God of our salvation, and cause thine anger toward us to cease. Wilt thou be angry with us for ever? wilt thou draw out thine anger to all generations?

Luke 5: 31 - 32
And Jesus answering said unto them, They that are whole need not a physician; but they that are sick. I came not to call the righteous, but sinners to repentance.

Isaiah 55: 7
Let the wicked forsake his way, and the unrighteous man his thoughts: and let him return unto the Lord, and he will have mercy upon him; and to our God, for he will abundantly pardon.

Ezekiel 18: 21
But if the wicked will turn from all his sins that he hath committed, and keep all my statutes, and do that which is lawful and right, he shall surely live, he shall not die.

Isaiah 30: 15
For thus saith the Lord God, the Holy One of Israel; In returning and rest shall ye be saved; in quietness and in confidence shall be your strength: and ye would not.

1 John 1: 9
If we confess our sins, he is faithful and just to forgive us our sins, and to cleanse us from all unrighteousness.

Acts 3: 26
Unto you first God, having raised up his Son Jesus, sent him to bless you, in turning away every one of you from his iniquities.

Psalm 34: 18
The Lord is nigh unto them that are of a broken heart; and saveth such as be of a contrite spirit.

Acts 3: 19 - 21
Repent ye therefore, and be converted, that your sins may be blotted out, when the times of refreshing shall come from the presence of the Lord; And he shall send Jesus Christ, which before was preached unto you: Whom the heaven must receive until the times of restitution of all things, which God hath spoken by the mouth of all his holy prophets since the world began.

2 Chronicles 7: 14
If my people, which are called by my name, shall humble themselves, and pray, and seek my face, and turn from their wicked ways; then will I hear from heaven, and will forgive their sin, and will heal their land.

Rewards

*"Never underestimate the power of dreams
and the influence of the human spirit.
We are all the same in this notion:
The potential for greatness lives within each of us."*

– Wilma Rudolph

Mark 10: 29 - 31
And Jesus answered and said, Verily I say unto you, There is no man that hath left house, or brethren, or sisters, or father, or mother, or wife, or children, or lands, for my sake, and the gospel's, - But he shall receive an hundredfold now in this time, houses, and brethren, and sisters, and mothers, and children, and lands, with persecutions; and in the world to come eternal life. But many that are first shall be last; and the last first.

Jeremiah 17: 10
I the Lord search the heart, I try the reins, even to give every man according to his ways, and according to the fruit of his doings.

1 Corinthians 3: 10 -- 14

According to the grace of God which is given unto me, as a wise masterbuilder, I have laid the foundation, and another buildeth thereon. But let every man take heed how he buildeth thereupon. For other foundation can no man lay than that is laid, which is Jesus Christ. Now if any man build upon this foundation gold, silver, precious stones, wood, hay, stubble; Every man's work shall be made manifest: for the day shall declare it, because it shall be revealed by fire; and the fire shall try every man's work of what sort it is. If any man's work abide which he hath built thereupon, he shall receive a reward.

Ephesians 6: 8

Knowing that whatsoever good thing any man doeth, the same shall he receive of the Lord, whether he be bond or free.

Matthew 10: 42

And whosoever shall give to drink unto one of these little ones a cup of cold water only in the name of a disciple, verily I say unto you, he shall in no wise lose his reward.

2 John 8 - 9

Look to yourselves, that we lose not those things which we have wrought, but that we receive a full reward. Whosoever transgresseth, and abideth not in the doctrine of Christ, hath not God. He that abideth in the doctrine of Christ, he hath both the Father and the Son.

Luke 12: 32

Fear not, little flock; for it is your Father's good pleasure to give you the kingdom.

Proverbs 21: 21
He that followeth after righteousness and mercy findeth life, righteousness, and honour.

Luke 18: 29 - 30
And he said unto them, Verily I say unto you, There is no man that hath left house, or parents, or brethren, or wife, or children, for the kingdom of God's sake, Who shall not receive manifold more in this present time, and in the world to come life everlasting.

1 John 2: 17
And the world passeth away, and the lust thereof: but he that doeth the will of God abideth for ever.

Psalm 31: 23
O love the Lord, all ye his saints: for the Lord preserveth the faithful, and plentifully rewardeth the proud doer.

Luke 6: 35
But love ye your enemies, and do good, and lend, hoping for nothing again; and your reward shall be great, and ye shall be the children of the Highest: for he is kind unto the unthankful and to the evil.

Righteousness

My dear sister, take note of this: Everyone should be quick to listen, slow to speak and slow to become angry, for man's anger does not bring about the righteous life that God desires.

— Beverly Sills

Psalm 145: 16 - 19
Thou openest thine hand, and satisfiest the desire of every living thing. The Lord is righteous in all his ways, and holy in all his works. The Lord is nigh unto all them that call upon him, to all that call upon him in truth. He will fulfill the desire of them that fear him: he also will hear their cry, and will save them.

Matthew 5: 10
Blessed are they which are persecuted for righteousness' sake: for theirs is the kingdom of heaven.

Proverbs 10: 24 - 25
The fear of the wicked, it shall come upon him: but the desire of the righteous shall be granted. As the whirlwind passeth, so is the wicked no more: but the righteous is an everlasting foundation.

Psalm 112: 1 - 3
Praise ye the Lord. Blessed is the man that feareth the Lord, that delighteth greatly in his commandments. His seed shall be mighty upon earth: the generation of the upright shall be blessed. Wealth and riches shall be in his house: and his righteousness endureth for ever.

Proverbs 16: 8
Better is a little with righteousness than great revenues without right.

Psalm 112: 5 - 6
A good man sheweth favour, and lendeth: he will guide his affairs with discretion. Surely he shall not be moved for ever: the righteous shall be in everlasting remembrance.

Matthew 5: 6
Blessed are they which do hunger and thirst after righteousness: for they shall be filled.

Proverbs 10: 2
Hatred stirreth up strifes: but love covereth all sins.

Isaiah 32: 17
And the work of righteousness shall be peace; and the effect of righteousness quietness and assurance for ever.

2 Corinthians 5: 21
For he hath made him to be sin for us, who knew no sin; that we might be made the righteousness of God in him.

1 John 2: 1 - 2
My little children, these things write I unto you, that ye sin not. And if any man sin, we have an advocate with the Father, Jesus Christ the righteous: And he is the propitiation for our sins: and not for ours only, but also for the sins of the whole world.

Proverbs 21: 21
He that followeth after righteousness and mercy findeth life, righteousness, and honour.

Psalm 94: 14 - 15
For the Lord will not cast off his people, neither will he forsake his inheritance. But judgment shall return unto righteousness: and all the upright in heart shall follow it.

Romans 5: 18 - 19
Therefore as by the offence of one judgment came upon all men to condemnation; even so by the righteousness of one the free gift came upon all men unto justification of life.
For as by one man's disobedience many were made sinners, so by the obedience of one shall many be made righteous.

Proverbs 28: 1
The wicked flee when no man pursueth: but the righteous are bold as a lion.

Psalm 84: 11
For the Lord God is a sun and shield: the Lord will give grace and glory: no good thing will he withhold from them that walk uprightly.

Romans 3: 21 - 22
But now the righteousness of God without the law is manifested, being witnessed by the law and the prophets; Even the righteousness of God which is by faith of Jesus Christ unto all and upon all them that believe: for there is no difference:

Salvation

There's much more for me included in Christ's
salvation than merely a paid ticket to heaven.
There is victory over present circumstances
if I am willing to accept it.

— Matilda Nordtvedt

Salvation is all-encompassing.
It is our healing, our preservation, our protection,
our welfare, our deliverance, our health, our help.
God, in His infinite wisdom and power and mercy,
knew that we needed to be saved from sickness,
disease, calamity, bondage, and the ultimate — eternal
death. Christ came and saved us from everything
that is ungodly, everything that is not like Him.
This is our salvation. Jesus, Hebrew for Joshua
or yeshua, means "salvation."
He is our salvation.

— C. Byrd

Psalm 91: 14 - 16

Because he hath set his love upon me, therefore will I deliver him: I will set him on high, because he hath known my name. He shall call upon me, and I will answer him: I will be with him in trouble; I will deliver him, and honour him. With long life will I satisfy him, and shew him my salvation.

1 Timothy 2: 5 - 6

For there is one God, and one mediator between God and men, the man Christ Jesus; Who gave himself a ransom for all, to be testified in due time.

Psalm 3: 8

Salvation belongeth unto the Lord: thy blessing is upon thy people. Selah.

Psalm 34: 7

The angel of the Lord encampeth round about them that fear him, and delivereth them.

2 Corinthians 6: 2

For he saith, I have heard thee in a time accepted, and in the day of salvation have I succoured thee: behold, now is the accepted time; behold, now is the day of salvation.

Acts 10: 43

To him give all the prophets witness, that through his name whosoever believeth in him shall receive remission of sins.

Mark 16: 16

He that believeth and is baptized shall be saved; but he that believeth not shall be damned.

Hebrews 5: 9
And being made perfect, he became the author of eternal salvation unto all them that obey him;

Isaiah 45: 22
Look unto me, and be ye saved, all the ends of the earth: for I am God, and there is none else.

Romans 10: 9 - 10
That if thou shalt confess with thy mouth the Lord Jesus, and shalt believe in thine heart that God hath raised him from the dead, thou shalt be saved. For with the heart man believeth unto righteousness; and with the mouth confession is made unto salvation.

Exodus 15: 2
The Lord is my strength and song, and he is become my salvation: he is my God, and I will prepare him an habitation; my father's God, and I will exalt him.

1 John 4: 10
Herein is love, not that we loved God, but that he loved us, and sent his Son to be the propitiation for our sins.

Psalm 33: 18 - 19
Behold, the eye of the Lord is upon them that fear him, upon them that hope in his mercy; To deliver their soul from death, and to keep them alive in famine.

John 3: 16 - 17
For God so loved the world, that he gave his only begotten Son, that whosoever believeth in him should not perish, but have

everlasting life. For God sent not his Son into the world to condemn the world; but that the world through him might be saved.

John 10: 9

I am the door: by me if any man enter in, he shall be saved, and shall go in and out, and find pasture.

Exodus 14: 13

And Moses said unto the people, Fear ye not, stand still, and see the salvation of the Lord, which he will shew to you to day: for the Egyptians whom ye have seen to day, ye shall see them again no more for ever.

Romans 3: 23 - 26

Being justified freely by his grace through the redemption that is in Christ Jesus:
Whom God hath set forth to be a propitiation through faith in his blood, to declare his righteousness for the remission of sins that are past, through the forbearance of God; To declare, I say, at this time his righteousness: that he might be just, and the justifier of him which believeth in Jesus.

Hebrews 9: 28

So Christ was once offered to bear the sins of many; and unto them that look for him shall he appear the second time without sin unto salvation.

Romans 5: 8 - 9

But God commendeth his love toward us, in that, while we were yet sinners, Christ died for us. Much more then, being now justified by his blood, we shall be saved from wrath through him.

Matthew 26: 26 - 28

And as they were eating, Jesus took bread, and blessed it, and brake it, and gave it to the disciples, and said, Take, eat; this is my body. And he took the cup, and gave thanks, and gave it to them, saying, Drink ye all of it; For this is my blood of the new testament, which is shed for many for the remission of sins.

Ephesians 2: 13 - 14

But now in Christ Jesus ye who sometimes were far off are made nigh by the blood of Christ. For he is our peace, who hath made both one, and hath broken down the middle wall of partition between us;

1 John 2: 1 - 2

My little children, these things write I unto you, that ye sin not. And if any man sin, we have an advocate with the Father, Jesus Christ the righteous: And he is the propitiation for our sins: and not for ours only, but also for the sins of the whole world.

2 Corinthians 5: 21

For he hath made him to be sin for us, who knew no sin; that we might be made the righteousness of God in him.

1 Peter 2: 21, 24 - 25

For even hereunto were ye called: because Christ also suffered for us, leaving us an example, that ye should follow his steps: For ye were as sheep going astray; but are now returned unto the Shepherd and Bishop of your souls.
For even hereunto were ye called: because Christ also suffered for us, leaving us an example, that ye should follow his steps:

Hebrews 9: 13 - 14

For if the blood of bulls and of goats, and the ashes of an heifer sprinkling the unclean, sanctifieth to the purifying of the flesh: How much more shall the blood of Christ, who through the eternal Spirit offered himself without spot to God, purge your conscience from dead works to serve the living God?

1 Peter 1: 18 - 19

Forasmuch as ye know that ye were not redeemed with corruptible things, as silver and gold, from your vain conversation received by tradition from your fathers; But with the precious blood of Christ, as of a lamb without blemish and without spot:

Psalm 37: 39

But the salvation of the righteous is of the Lord: he is their strength in the time of trouble.

Colossians 2: 13 - 14

And you, being dead in your sins and the uncircumcision of your flesh, hath he quickened together with him, having forgiven you all trespasses; Blotting out the handwriting of ordinances that was against us, which was contrary to us, and took it out of the way, nailing it to his cross;

Psalm 62: 1 - 2

Truly my soul waiteth upon God: from him cometh my salvation. He only is my rock and my salvation; he is my defence; I shall not be greatly moved.

Self Esteem

"Think like a queen. A queen is not afraid to fail. Failure is another steppingstone to greatness."

– Oprah Winfrey

Isaiah 49: 15 - 16
Can a woman forget her sucking child, that she should not have compassion on the son of her womb? yea, they may forget, yet will I not forget thee. Behold, I have graven thee upon the palms of my hands; thy walls are continually before me.

Ephesians 2: 10
For we are his workmanship, created in Christ Jesus unto good works, which God hath before ordained that we should walk in them.

Hebrews 10: 35
Cast not away therefore your confidence, which hath great recompence of reward.

Hebrews 13: 6
So that we may boldly say, The Lord is my helper, and I will not fear what man shall do unto me.

Isaiah 43: 4
Since thou wast precious in my sight, thou hast been honourable, and I have loved thee: therefore will I give men for thee, and people for thy life.

Matthew 10: 29 - 31
Are not two sparrows sold for a farthing? and one of them shall not fall on the ground without your Father. But the very hairs of your head are all numbered. Fear ye not therefore, ye are of more value than many sparrows.

Ephesians 1: 3 - 6
Blessed be the God and Father of our Lord Jesus Christ, who hath blessed us with all spiritual blessings in heavenly places in Christ: According as he hath chosen us in him before the foundation of the world, that we should be holy and without blame before him in love: Having predestinated us unto the adoption of children by Jesus Christ to himself, according to the good pleasure of his will, To the praise of the glory of his grace, wherein he hath made us accepted in the beloved.

Jeremiah 31: 3
The Lord hath appeared of old unto me, saying, Yea, I have loved thee with an everlasting love: therefore with lovingkindness have I drawn thee.

2 Corinthians 12: 9
And he said unto me, My grace is sufficient for thee: for my strength is made perfect in weakness. Most gladly therefore will I rather glory in my infirmities, that the power of Christ may rest upon me.

Hebrews 10: 19, 22
Having therefore, brethren, boldness to enter into the holiest by the blood of Jesus, Let us draw near with a true heart in full assurance of faith, having our hearts sprinkled from an evil conscience, and our bodies washed with pure water.

Psalm 27: 1, 3
The Lord is my light and my salvation; whom shall I fear? the Lord is the strength of my life; of whom shall I be afraid? Though an host should encamp against me, my heart shall not fear: though war should rise against me, in this will I be confident.

Psalm 18: 2 - 3
The Lord is my rock, and my fortress, and my deliverer; my God, my strength, in whom I will trust; my buckler, and the horn of my salvation, and my high tower. I will call upon the Lord, who is worthy to be praised: so shall I be saved from mine enemies.

Jeremiah 17: 7 - 8
Blessed is the man that trusteth in the Lord, and whose hope the Lord is. For he shall be as a tree planted by the waters, and that spreadeth out her roots by the river, and shall not see when heat cometh, but her leaf shall be green; and shall not be careful in the year of drought, neither shall cease from yielding fruit.

Psalm 119: 73
Thy hands have made me and fashioned me:
give me understanding, that I may learn thy
commandments.

1 John 3: 21 - 22
Beloved, if our heart condemn us not, then have we
confidence toward God. And whatsoever we ask, we
receive of him, because we keep his commandments, and
do those things that are pleasing in his sight.

Psalm 139: 13 - 14
For thou hast possessed my reins: thou hast covered me
in my mother's womb. I will praise thee; for I am fearfully
and wonderfully made: marvellous are thy works; and
that my soul knoweth right well.

Psalm 100: 3
Know ye that the Lord he is God: it is he that hath made
us, and not we ourselves; we are his people, and the sheep
of his pasture.

Strength

"You may encounter many defeats, but you must not be defeated. In fact, it may be necessary to encounter the defeats, so you can know who you are, what you can rise from, how you can still come out of it."

– Maya Angelou

Isaiah 40: 29 - 31
He giveth power to the faint; and to them that have no might he increaseth strength. Even the youths shall faint and be weary, and the young men shall utterly fall: But they that wait upon the Lord shall renew their strength; they shall mount up with wings as eagles; they shall run, and not be weary; and they shall walk, and not faint.

Psalm 20: 6
Now know I that the Lord saveth his anointed; he will hear him from his holy heaven with the saving strength of his right hand.

Deuteronomy 31: 6
Be strong and of a good courage, fear not, nor be afraid of them: for the Lord thy God, he it is that doth go with thee; he will not fail thee, nor forsake thee.

Psalm 46: 1
God is our refuge and strength, a very present help in trouble.

Isaiah 41: 10
Fear thou not; for I am with thee: be not dismayed; for I am thy God: I will strengthen thee; yea, I will help thee; yea, I will uphold thee with the right hand of my righteousness.

Psalm 18: 1 - 2
I will love thee, O Lord, my strength. The Lord is my rock, and my fortress, and my deliverer; my God, my strength, in whom I will trust; my buckler, and the horn of my salvation, and my high tower.

Isaiah 50: 7
For the Lord God will help me; therefore shall I not be confounded: therefore have I set my face like a flint, and I know that I shall not be ashamed.

Proverbs 3: 25 - 26
Be not afraid of sudden fear, neither of the desolation of the wicked, when it cometh. For the Lord shall be thy confidence, and shall keep thy foot from being taken.

Psalm 18: 28 - 29
For thou wilt light my candle: the Lord my God will enlighten my darkness. For by thee I have run through a troop; and by my God have I leaped over a wall.

Psalm 31: 23 - 24

O love the Lord, all ye his saints: for the Lord preserveth the faithful, and plentifully rewardeth the proud doer. Be of good courage, and he shall strengthen your heart, all ye that hope in the Lord.

Psalm 27: 1 - 3

The Lord is my light and my salvation; whom shall I fear? the Lord is the strength of my life; of whom shall I be afraid? When the wicked, even mine enemies and my foes, came upon me to eat up my flesh, they stumbled and fell. Though an host should encamp against me, my heart shall not fear: though war should rise against me, in this will I be confident.

Psalm 84: 5

Blessed is the man whose strength is in thee; in whose heart are the ways of them.

Success

*"There is no royal flower-strewn path to success.
And if there is, I have not found it
for if I have accomplished anything in life
it is because I have been willing to work hard."*

— Madam C.J. Walker, Walker Cosmetics line

Proverbs 22: 4
Our fathers trusted in thee: they trusted, and thou didst deliver them.

Psalm 1: 1 - 3
Blessed is the man that walketh not in the counsel of the ungodly, nor standeth in the way of sinners, nor sitteth in the seat of the scornful. But his delight is in the law of the Lord; and in his law doth he meditate day and night. And he shall be like a tree planted by the rivers of water, that bringeth forth his fruit in his season; his leaf also shall not wither; and whatsoever he doeth shall prosper.

Psalm 20: 1, 4
The Lord hear thee in the day of trouble; the name of the God of Jacob defend thee; Grant thee according to thine own heart, and fulfil all thy counsel.

Proverbs 8: 18 - 21
Riches and honour are with me; yea, durable riches and righteousness. My fruit is better than gold, yea, than fine gold; and my revenue than choice silver. I lead in the way of righteousness, in the midst of the paths of judgment: That I may cause those that love me to inherit substance; and I will fill their treasures.

2 Chronicles 20: 20
And they rose early in the morning, and went forth into the wilderness of Tekoa: and as they went forth, Jehoshaphat stood and said, Hear me, O Judah, and ye inhabitants of Jerusalem; Believe in the Lord your God, so shall ye be established; believe his prophets, so shall ye prosper.

Proverbs 28: 13
He that covereth his sins shall not prosper: but whoso confesseth and forsaketh them shall have mercy.

Psalm 75: 6 - 7
For promotion cometh neither from the east, nor from the west, nor from the south. But God is the judge: he putteth down one, and setteth up another.

Deuteronomy 28: 1 - 2, 8
And it shall come to pass, if thou shalt hearken diligently unto the voice of the Lord thy God, to observe and to do all his commandments which I command thee this day, that the Lord

thy God will set thee on high above all nations of the earth: And all these blessings shall come on thee, and overtake thee, if thou shalt hearken unto the voice of the Lord thy God. The Lord shall command the blessing upon thee in thy storehouses, and in all that thou settest thine hand unto; and he shall bless thee in the land which the Lord thy God giveth thee.

Joshua 1: 8
This book of the law shall not depart out of thy mouth; but thou shalt meditate therein day and night, that thou mayest observe to do according to all that is written therein: for then thou shalt make thy way prosperous, and then thou shalt have good success.

Psalm 35: 27
Let them shout for joy, and be glad, that favour my righteous cause: yea, let them say continually, Let the Lord be magnified, which hath pleasure in the prosperity of his servant.

Proverb 15: 22
Without counsel purposes are disappointed: but in the multitude of counsellors they are established.

Proverbs 16: 3
Commit thy works unto the Lord, and thy thoughts shall be established.

Isaiah 25: 8 - 9
He will swallow up death in victory; and the Lord God will wipe away tears from off all faces; and the rebuke of his people shall he take away from off all the earth: for the Lord hath spoken it. And it shall be said in that day, Lo, this is our God; we have waited for him, and he will save us: this is the Lord; we have waited for him, we will be glad and rejoice in his salvation.

Matthew 12: 20
A bruised reed shall he not break, and smoking flax shall he not quench, till he send forth judgment unto victory.

Psalm 98: 1
O sing unto the Lord a new song; for he hath done marvellous things: his right hand, and his holy arm, hath gotten him the victory.

Proverbs 10: 4
He becometh poor that dealeth with a slack hand: but the hand of the diligent maketh rich.

1 John 5: 4 - 5
For whatsoever is born of God overcometh the world: and this is the victory that overcometh the world, even our faith. Who is he that overcometh the world, but he that believeth that Jesus is the Son of God?

1 Corinthians 15: 52, 54 - 57
In a moment, in the twinkling of an eye, at the last trump: for the trumpet shall sound, and the dead shall be raised incorruptible, and we shall be changed. So when this corruptible shall have put on incorruption, and this mortal shall have put on immortality, then shall be brought to pass the saying that is written, Death is swallowed up in victory.
O death, where is thy sting? O grave, where is thy victory? The sting of death is sin; and the strength of sin is the law. But thanks be to God, which giveth us the victory through our Lord Jesus Christ.

Thankfulness

"Be thankful for what you have; you'll end up having more. If you concentrate on what you don't have, you will never, ever have enough."

— Oprah Winfrey, first hugely successful African-American woman in media

Psalm 30: 11 - 12
Thou hast turned for me my mourning into dancing: thou hast put off my sackcloth, and girded me with gladness; To the end that my glory may sing praise to thee, and not be silent. O Lord my God, I will give thanks unto thee for ever.

1 Thessalonians 5: 18
In every thing give thanks: for this is the will of God in Christ Jesus concerning you.

Psalm 107: 1
O give thanks unto the Lord, for he is good: for his mercy endureth for ever.

1 Timothy 2: 1 - 3
O give thanks unto the Lord; for he is good: for his mercy endureth for ever. O give thanks unto the God of gods: for his mercy endureth for ever. O give thanks to the Lord of lords: for his mercy endureth for ever.

Psalm 69: 30 - 32
I will praise the name of God with a song, and will magnify him with thanksgiving. This also shall please the Lord better than an ox or bullock that hath horns and hoofs. The humble shall see this, and be glad: and your heart shall live that seek God.

1 Corinthians 15: 57
But thanks be to God, which giveth us the victory through our Lord Jesus Christ.

Psalm 95: 2, 7
Let us come before his presence with thanksgiving, and make a joyful noise unto him with psalms. For he is our God; and we are the people of his pasture, and the sheep of his hand. To day if ye will hear his voice,

Isaiah 63: 7 - 8
I will mention the lovingkindnesses of the Lord, and the praises of the Lord, according to all that the Lord hath bestowed on us, and the great goodness toward the house of Israel, which he hath bestowed on them according to his mercies, and according to the multitude of his lovingkindnesses. For he said, Surely they are my people, children that will not lie: so he was their Saviour.

Ephesians 1: 16 - 17
Cease not to give thanks for you, making mention of you in my prayers; That the God of our Lord Jesus Christ, the Father of glory, may give unto you the spirit of wisdom and revelation in the knowledge of him:

2 Thessalonians 2: 13 - 14
But we are bound to give thanks alway to God for you, brethren beloved of the Lord, because God hath from the beginning chosen you to salvation through sanctification of the Spirit and belief of the truth: Whereunto he called you by our gospel, to the obtaining of the glory of our Lord Jesus Christ.

Psalm 100: 4 - 5
Enter into his gates with thanksgiving, and into his courts with praise: be thankful unto him, and bless his name. For the Lord is good; his mercy is everlasting; and his truth endureth to all generations.

1 Timothy 4: 4 - 5
For every creature of God is good, and nothing to be refused, if it be received with thanksgiving: For it is sanctified by the word of God and prayer.

2 Corinthians 2: 14
Now thanks be unto God, which always causeth us to triumph in Christ, and maketh manifest the savour of his knowledge by us in every place.

Colossians 2: 6 - 7

As ye have therefore received Christ Jesus the Lord, so walk ye in him: Rooted and built up in him, and stablished in the faith, as ye have been taught, abounding therein with thanksgiving.

Revelation 7: 12

Saying, Amen: Blessing, and glory, and wisdom, and thanksgiving, and honour, and power, and might, be unto our God for ever and ever. Amen.

Hebrews 13: 15 - 16

By him therefore let us offer the sacrifice of praise to God continually, that is, the fruit of our lips giving thanks to his name. But to do good and to communicate forget not: for with such sacrifices God is well pleased.

Philippians 4: 5 - 7

Let your moderation be known unto all men. The Lord is at hand. Be careful for nothing; but in every thing by prayer and supplication with thanksgiving let your requests be made known unto God. And the peace of God, which passeth all understanding, shall keep your hearts and minds through Christ Jesus.

Truth

*"In every crisis there is a message.
Crises are nature's way of forcing change — breaking
down old structures, shaking loose negative habits
so that something new and better
can take their place."*

— Susan L. Taylor

John 18: 37
Pilate therefore said unto him, Art thou a king then? Jesus answered, Thou sayest that I am a king. To this end was I born, and for this cause came I into the world, that I should bear witness unto the truth. Every one that is of the truth heareth my voice.

1 John 5: 20
And we know that the Son of God is come, and hath given us an understanding, that we may know him that is true, and we are in him that is true, even in his Son Jesus Christ. This is the true God, and eternal life.

Psalm 15: 1 - 2
Lord, who shall abide in thy tabernacle? who shall dwell in thy holy hill? He that walketh uprightly, and worketh righteousness, and speaketh the truth in his heart.

Psalm 145: 18
The Lord is nigh unto all them that call upon him, to all that call upon him in truth.

Proverbs 12: 17
He that speaketh truth sheweth forth righteousness: but a false witness deceit.

John 14: 6
Jesus saith unto him, I am the way, the truth, and the life: no man cometh unto the Father, but by me.

Psalm 119: 160
Thy word is true from the beginning: and every one of thy righteous judgments endureth for ever.

Isaiah 33: 15 - 16
He that walketh righteously, and speaketh uprightly; he that despiseth the gain of oppressions, that shaketh his hands from holding of bribes, that stoppeth his ears from hearing of blood, and shutteth his eyes from seeing evil; He shall dwell on high: his place of defence shall be the munitions of rocks: bread shall be given him; his waters shall be sure.

John 8: 32
And ye shall know the truth, and the truth shall make you free.

Psalm 33: 4 - 5
For the word of the Lord is right; and all his works are done in truth. He loveth righteousness and judgment: the earth is full of the goodness of the Lord.

Proverbs 14: 25
A true witness delivereth souls: but a deceitful witness speaketh lies.

Jeremiah 10: 10
But the Lord is the true God, he is the living God, and an everlasting king: at his wrath the earth shall tremble, and the nations shall not be able to abide his indignation.

Psalm 19: 9 - 10
The fear of the Lord is clean, enduring for ever: the judgments of the Lord are true and righteous altogether. More to be desired are they than gold, yea, than much fine gold: sweeter also than honey and the honeycomb.

Proverbs 12: 22
Lying lips are abomination to the Lord: but they that deal truly are his delight.

Philippians 4: 8 - 9
Finally, brethren, whatsoever things are true, whatsoever things are honest, whatsoever things are just, whatsoever things are pure, whatsoever things are lovely, whatsoever things are of good report; if there be any virtue, and if there be any praise, think on these things. Those things, which ye have both learned, and received, and heard, and seen in me, do: and the God of peace shall be with you.

Psalm 86: 15
But thou, O Lord, art a God full of compassion, and gracious, longsuffering, and plenteous in mercy and truth.

Proverbs 16: 24
Pleasant words are as an honeycomb, sweet to the soul, and health to the bones.

1 Peter 4: 11
If any man speak, let him speak as the oracles of God; if any man minister, let him do it as of the ability which God giveth: that God in all things may be glorified through Jesus Christ, to whom be praise and dominion for ever and ever. Amen.

Luke 8: 4 - 5, 8, 11, 15
And when much people were gathered together, and were come to him out of every city, he spake by a parable: A sower went out to sow his seed: and as he sowed, some fell by the way side; and it was trodden down, and the fowls of the air devoured it. And other fell on good ground, and sprang up, and bare fruit an hundredfold. And when he had said these things, he cried, He that hath ears to hear, let him hear. Now the parable is this: The seed is the word of God. But that on the good ground are they, which in an honest and good heart, having heard the word, keep it, and bring forth fruit with patience.

Ecclesiastes 9: 17
The words of wise men are heard in quiet more than the cry of him that ruleth among fools.

Proverbs 21: 23
Whoso keepeth his mouth and his tongue keepeth his soul from troubles.

Proverbs 10: 9
He that walketh uprightly walketh surely: but he that perverteth his ways shall be known.

Proverbs 24: 26
Every man shall kiss his lips that giveth a right answer.

Proverbs 15: 4
A wholesome tongue is a tree of life: but perverseness therein is a breach in the spirit.

Ephesians 4: 15
But speaking the truth in love, may grow up into him in all things, which is the head, even Christ:

John 16: 13
Howbeit when he, the Spirit of truth, is come, he will guide you into all truth: for he shall not speak of himself; but whatsoever he shall hear, that shall he speak: and he will shew you things to come.

Wisdom

"There's a beauty to wisdom and experience that cannot be faked. It's impossible to be mature without having lived."

— Amy Grant singer

Proverbs 3: 13 - 14
Happy is the man that findeth wisdom, and the man that getteth understanding. For the merchandise of it is better than the merchandise of silver, and the gain thereof than fine gold.

Ecclesiastes 7: 19
Wisdom strengtheneth the wise more than ten mighty men which are in the city.

Psalm 90: 12
So teach us to number our days, that we may apply our hearts unto wisdom.

Proverbs 11: 2
When pride cometh, then cometh shame: but with the lowly is wisdom.

James 1: 5
If any of you lack wisdom, let him ask of God, that giveth to all men liberally, and upbraideth not; and it shall be given him.

Proverbs 4: 7 - 8
Wisdom is the principal thing; therefore get wisdom: and with all thy getting get understanding. Exalt her, and she shall promote thee: she shall bring thee to honour, when thou dost embrace her.

Ecclesiastes 2: 26
For God giveth to a man that is good in his sight wisdom, and knowledge, and joy: but to the sinner he giveth travail, to gather and to heap up, that he may give to him that is good before God. This also is vanity and vexation of spirit.

Proverbs 2: 10
When wisdom entereth into thine heart, and knowledge is pleasant unto thy soul;

Proverbs 24: 14
So shall the knowledge of wisdom be unto thy soul: when thou hast found it, then there shall be a reward, and thy expectation shall not be cut off.

Proverbs 4: 10 - 13
Hear, O my son, and receive my sayings; and the years of thy life shall be many. I have taught thee in the way of wisdom; I have led thee in right paths. When thou goest, thy steps shall not be straitened; and when thou runnest, thou shalt not stumble. Take fast hold of instruction; let her not go: keep her; for she is thy life.

1 Corinthians 2: 12 - 16
Now we have received, not the spirit of the world, but the spirit which is of God; that we might know the things that are freely given to us of God. Which things also we speak, not in the words which man's wisdom teacheth, but which the Holy Ghost teacheth; comparing spiritual things with spiritual. But the natural man receiveth not the things of the Spirit of God: for they are foolishness unto him: neither can he know them, because they are spiritually discerned. But he that is spiritual judgeth all things, yet he himself is judged of no man. For who hath known the mind of the Lord, that he may instruct him? But we have the mind of Christ.

Proverbs 2: 6 - 7
For the Lord giveth wisdom: out of his mouth cometh knowledge and understanding. He layeth up sound wisdom for the righteous: he is a buckler to them that walk uprightly.

1 John 4: 6
Ye are of God, little children, and have overcome them: because greater is he that is in you, than he that is in the world.

Isaiah 30: 21
And thine ears shall hear a word behind thee, saying, This is the way, walk ye in it, when ye turn to the right hand, and when ye turn to the left.

Proverbs 19: 8
He that getteth wisdom loveth his own soul: he that keepeth understanding shall find good.

James 3: 17 - 18
But the wisdom that is from above is first pure, then peaceable, gentle, and easy to be intreated, full of mercy and good fruits, without partiality, and without hypocrisy. And the fruit of righteousness is sown in peace of them that make peace.

Ecclesiastes 7: 11 - 12
Wisdom is good with an inheritance: and by it there is profit to them that see the sun. For wisdom is a defence, and money is a defence: but the excellency of knowledge is, that wisdom giveth life to them that have it.

Psalm 51: 6
Behold, thou desirest truth in the inward parts: and in the hidden part thou shalt make me to know wisdom.

Ecclesiastes 8: 1
Who is as the wise man? and who knoweth the interpretation of a thing? a man's wisdom maketh his face to shine, and the boldness of his face shall be changed.

Psalm 111: 10
The fear of the Lord is the beginning of wisdom: a good understanding have all they that do his commandments: his praise endureth for ever.

Job 28: 20 - 21, 23
Whence then cometh wisdom? and where is the place of understanding? Seeing it is hid from the eyes of all living, and kept close from the fowls of the air. God understandeth the way thereof, and he knoweth the place thereof.

2 Timothy 2: 1 - 2, 7
Thou therefore, my son, be strong in the grace that is in Christ Jesus. And the things that thou hast heard of me among many witnesses, the same commit thou to faithful men, who shall be able to teach others also. Consider what I say; and the Lord give thee understanding in all things.

Ecclesiastes 8: 5
Whoso keepeth the commandment shall feel no evil thing: and a wise man's heart discerneth both time and judgment.

Working

"Nothing will work unless you do."
– Maya Angelou

Colossians 3: 23 - 24
And whatsoever ye do, do it heartily, as to the Lord, and not unto men; Knowing that of the Lord ye shall receive the reward of the inheritance: for ye serve the Lord Christ.

Proverbs 13: 11
Wealth gotten by vanity shall be diminished: but he that gathereth by labour shall increase.

Ecclesiastes 5: 18 - 19
Behold that which I have seen: it is good and comely for one to eat and to drink, and to enjoy the good of all his labour that he taketh under the sun all the days of his life, which God giveth him: for it is his portion. Every man also to whom God hath given riches and wealth, and hath given him power to eat thereof, and to take his portion, and to rejoice in his labour; this is the gift of God.

Proverbs 10: 4
He becometh poor that dealeth with a slack hand: but the hand of the diligent maketh rich.

1 Corinthians 15: 58
Therefore, my beloved brethren, be ye stedfast, unmovable, always abounding in the work of the Lord, forasmuch as ye know that your labour is not in vain in the Lord.

Psalm 62: 12
Also unto thee, O Lord, belongeth mercy: for thou renderest to every man according to his work.

John 6: 27
Labour not for the meat which perisheth, but for that meat which endureth unto everlasting life, which the Son of man shall give unto you: for him hath God the Father sealed.

2 Chronicles 15: 7
Be ye strong therefore, and let not your hands be weak: for your work shall be rewarded.

Matthew 11: 28
Come unto me, all ye that labour and are heavy laden, and I will give you rest.

Psalm 111: 3 - 4
His work is honourable and glorious: and his righteousness endureth for ever. He hath made his wonderful works to be remembered: the Lord is gracious and full of compassion.

Psalm 90: 16 - 17

Let thy work appear unto thy servants, and thy glory unto their children. And let the beauty of the Lord our God be upon us: and establish thou the work of our hands upon us; yea, the work of our hands establish thou it.

Colossians 1: 10 - 11

That ye might walk worthy of the Lord unto all pleasing, being fruitful in every good work, and increasing in the knowledge of God; Strengthened with all might, according to his glorious power, unto all patience and longsuffering with joyfulness;

Psalm 31: 23

O love the Lord, all ye his saints: for the Lord preserveth the faithful, and plentifully rewardeth the proud doer.

Luke 16: 10

He that is faithful in that which is least is faithful also in much: and he that is unjust in the least is unjust also in much.

Jeremiah 17: 10

But the Lord is the true God, he is the living God, and an everlasting king: at his wrath the earth shall tremble, and the nations shall not be able to abide his indignation.

1 Corinthians 3: 10 - 14

According to the grace of God which is given unto me, as a wise masterbuilder, I have laid the foundation, and another buildeth thereon. But let every man take heed how he buildeth thereupon. For other foundation can no man lay than that is laid, which is Jesus Christ. Now if any man build upon this foundation gold, silver, precious stones, wood, hay, stubble; Every man's work shall be made manifest: for the day shall declare it, because it shall be revealed by fire; and the fire shall try every man's work of what sort it is. If any man's work abide which he hath built thereupon, he shall receive a reward.

Titus 3: 5

Not by works of righteousness which we have done, but according to his mercy he saved us, by the washing of regeneration, and renewing of the Holy Ghost;

Hebrews 6: 10

For God is not unrighteous to forget your work and labour of love, which ye have shewed toward his name, in that ye have ministered to the saints, and do minister.

1 John 2: 17

And the world passeth away, and the lust thereof: but he that doeth the will of God abideth for ever.

2 Corinthians 9: 8

And God is able to make all grace abound toward you; that ye, always having all sufficiency in all things, may abound to every good work:

Joshua 1: 8
This book of the law shall not depart out of thy mouth; but thou shalt meditate therein day and night, that thou mayest observe to do according to all that is written therein: for then thou shalt make thy way prosperous, and then thou shalt have good success.

Isaiah 65: 22 -23
They shall not build, and another inhabit; they shall not plant, and another eat: for as the days of a tree are the days of my people, and mine elect shall long enjoy the work of their hands. They shall not labour in vain, nor bring forth for trouble; for they are the seed of the blessed of the Lord, and their offspring with them.

Contributors

A. Middleton

C. Belt

B. Whitaker

C. Richards

R. Haynes

A. Howell

C. Archibald

C. Byrd

D. Manns

L. Ammons

A. Simms

K. Haynes

J. Thompson

C. Swafford - Harris

C. William- Neal

Goals/Plans

....
....
....
....
....
....
....
....
....
....
....
....
....
....
....
....
....
....
....
....
....
....
....

Goals/Plans

Goals/Plans

Goals/Plans

Goals/Plans

Goals/Plans

Goals/Plans

Goals/Plans

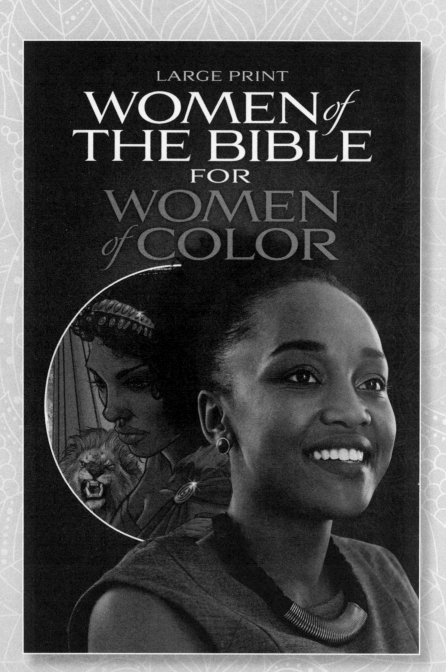

PROMISES FROM GOD FOR
MEN OF COLOR

THE NEW
Women of Color
DAILY DEVOTIONAL

FALL/WINTER EDITION

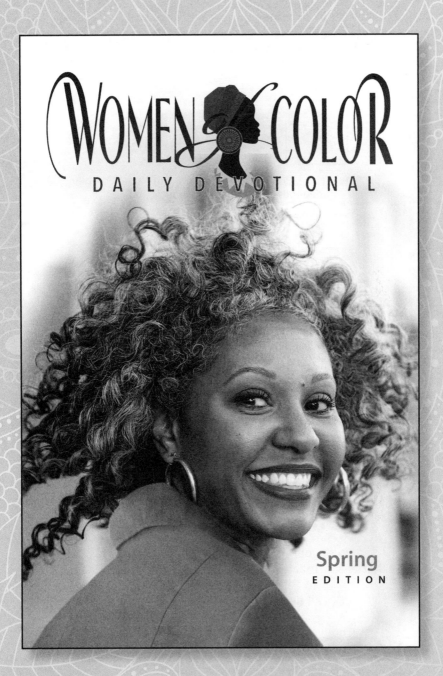

WOMEN ♦ COLOR
DAILY DEVOTIONAL

Spring
EDITION